# Comfort FOODS

# Comfort Foods

*America's Favorite Dishes,*
*Cooked the Way You Like Them*

## Rita M. Harris

PRIMA PUBLISHING

© 1996 by Rita M. Harris

Published by Prima Publishing, Roseville, California. Member of the Crown Publishing Group, a division of Random House, Inc.

Random House, Inc. New York, Toronto, London, Sydney, Auckland

PRIMA PUBLISHING and colophon are trademarks of Random House, Inc., registered with the United States Patent and Trademark Office.

**Library of Congress Cataloging-in-Publication Data**

Harris, Rita M.
  Comfort foods:  America's favorite dishes, cooked the way you like them / Rita M. Harris.
    p.    cm.
  Includes index.
  ISBN 0-7615-0629-2
  1. Cookery. I. Title.
TX714.H366 1996
641.5—dc20                                                        96-17241
                                                                       CIP

01 02 03 04 AA 11 10 9
Printed in the United States of America

First Edition

**Visit us online at www.primapublishing.com**

*To my beloved Bill,*

*who makes all things possible*

*and who believes in me.*

# CONTENTS

# FOREWORD

*T*his is life in a nutshell—you're born, someone slaps you, you cry, someone gives you milk, you stop crying. For as long as humans have been on the earth, food has been a source of comfort. And it's not just people; you've seen a dog "smile" after getting a treat, right?

Some psychologists will tell you that the most basic thing people seek is not money, sex, or thin thighs—it's comfort. But aren't comfort foods those bad foods that we are supposed to learn to live without? Maybe not.

Jim Fixx ate nothing but green vegetables for years, spent half his life running in those short shorts, and died before he was 50. James Beard was a giant of a man who made fresh bread everyday and ate it hot out of the oven slathered with butter. He lived to be 82. And who do you think had a better time?

OK, so maybe it had more to do with genetics than food—but what does that tell you? The truth is, no matter how little fat we eat or how much we exercise, we're all going to die sometime. When it's your time to go, you'll go. No one is sitting in heaven tabulating the grams of fat you've eaten so they can whisk you away when you reach a certain number. If they did, Julia Child would have died at 21 and Ghandi would have lived to be 150.

My mother always told me, "Enjoy today—you could be hit by a bus tomorrow." Those are words to live by, and they've never been more true.

It seems dietitians appear on the news every week telling us that Italian food is deadly or Mexican food is lethal. It's rumored that the next big announcement will be that even vegetables are toxic—after all, they contain pesticides and you could choke on them! If these things are true, then why did so many of our ancestors live long lives? Because they ate the comfort foods that made them happy, and being happy is good for you.

Don't get the wrong idea—comfort food isn't about gluttony—it's about the comfort and joy that certain special foods can bring to us. Eaten in moderation, even the richest foods can be healthful—not to mention emotionally and spiritually uplifting.

Everybody has a favorite comfort food. We tend to have sentimental feelings toward what we ate as a kid even if it came from "The Colonel." It reminds us of a time when other people took care of us and all we had to do was look both ways before crossing the street.

So while every recipe in this book may not press your particular comfort button, you'll surely find some that do. And when you do, treat yourself to the luxury of indulging yourself. You deserve it—we all do.

If you still feel too guilty about eating real food, then you can always tear out the pages of the book and suck on them. They're entirely fat-free and besides, unless you try it, you'll never know what flavor ink we used!

Daniel Will-Harris

# ACKNOWLEDGMENTS

*I* am grateful to Prima Publishing for enabling me to fulfill a lifelong dream of being a published writer. I want to offer special thanks to Jennifer Basye Sander, who "discovered" me;  to Alice Anderson, who always has a smile in her voice and offers great encouragement; to Debra Venzke, an endlessly patient, helpful, and constructive project editor; and Karen Fraley, copy editor. Stand up and take a bow, all you great ladies!

Thanks also to my son Daniel for writing the foreword to my book, and to all my children and grandchildren—Lisa, Loren, Howard, Catherine, Daniel, Toni, Ocea, Ari, Richard, and Alexander—for loving me and my cooking.

# INTRODUCTION

*M*y chief qualification for writing this book is that *I love food.* I love the taste, the textures, the flavors, the spices—even the blandness of food.

In my almost 70 years, I've done some serious eating. My favorite foods are the simple foods that bring comfort. I eat when I am happy, sad, or lonely, when I am in a crowd, when it's cold, and when it's hot. I estimate that I have eaten my body weight in food a dozen times and I still love food!

I've questioned literally hundreds of people about their food preferences. I ask, "What food would you choose if you needed only to put out your hand and have it appear—no shopping, no expenditure, no preparation?"

No one has indicated a preference for nouvelle cuisine or exotic creatures. I have included recipes in this book for the comfort foods that most people dream about.

If you have to be conscious of calories, cholesterol, or fat, this book should be considered a "wish book." One day the FDA will grant permission for the use of something like Olestra that will allow high-calorie foods to pass through the digestive system without being absorbed. Until that heavenly day, you will either need to modify these recipes, eat the paper pages, or just dream.

# APPETIZERS

$\mathcal{M}$y dear friend Lillian Fisher confided to me that when she eats in a restaurant, she prefers ordering appetizers rather than a meal. I agree with her. Consider the following recipes as snack food—the staff of life. They are impressive to serve and great to make for parties.

# GUACAMOLE

*A*vocado lovers, this is for you. This is perfectly delicious served with chips and any Mexican food.

**Serves 12**

### Ingredients

3 very ripe avocados, mashed

1 package (3 ounces) cream cheese, softened

1 small onion, finely chopped

1 large tomato, peeled and chopped

2 tablespoons chopped green chiles

1 tablespoon olive oil

Pinch of salt

Pepper to taste

Mix all the ingredients together until the mixture is creamy and smooth. If you do not serve this immediately, place the guacamole in a bowl with the pit of the avocado. Cover and refrigerate. This will keep the guacamole from becoming discolored.

Serve with corn or tortilla chips.

# TUNA PÂTÉ

## Ingredients

1 can (7 ounces) tuna,
  undrained
Pinch of pepper
Pinch of dill weed
1 package (8 ounces)
  cream cheese, at room
  temperature
2 hard boiled eggs
3 tablespoons chopped
  nuts, optional

*T*una is one of my favorite comfort foods. This is good with crackers or toast or served in the center of a bowl of finely sliced lettuce as a salad.

**Makes 2 cups**

Blend together the tuna and seasonings. Add the cream cheese and eggs and process until smooth. Chill. Garnish with the nuts.

# DEVILED EGGS

*T*here are lots of interesting ways to prepare deviled eggs. This is my favorite. You can eliminate the shrimp and add a tablespoon of chopped dill pickle, crushed anchovies, bits of ham—whatever you like.

**Serves 4**

Remove the egg yolks and mash them with a fork or press them through a sieve. Mix the shrimp and egg yolks together with the mayonnaise and season to taste.

Use a pastry tube or a spoon to fill the egg whites with the egg yolk mixture. Sprinkle with paprika and garnish with sprigs of parsley.

## Ingredients

4 hard boiled eggs, cut in
  half lengthwise
4 ounces cooked salad
  shrimp
$1/2$ cup mayonnaise
Salt and pepper to taste
Paprika or parsley sprigs
  for garnish

# KOSHER DILL PICKLES

## Ingredients

4 quarts water

¾ cup coarse or kosher salt

25 small pickling
     cucumbers

15 whole cloves garlic,
     peeled

1 bunch of fresh dill

4 bay leaves

1 teaspoon dill seeds

1 teaspoon whole black
     peppercorns

1 teaspoon mustard seeds

*C*runchy, garlic-flavored kosher dills are still served in crocks on the tables of famous Jewish delis. Making your own isn't difficult. Choose the small pickling cucumbers because the large ones get pulpy. You'll also need a wide-mouthed glass or ceramic crock. This recipe is at least 100 years old, so you know it's good.

**Makes 25 pickles**

Bring the water to a boil and add the salt, stirring until the salt is dissolved. Remove from heat and let the water cool for 30 minutes.

Scrub the cucumbers clean and set aside. Place the remaining ingredients in a large crock. Add the cucumbers to the crock. Pour in the salt water, making sure that it covers the cucumbers by a few inches. Place a plate over the top of the crock and weight it with a coffee mug filled with water. Set the crock in a cool place and cover it with cheesecloth.

Check the crock daily and skim off any foam that rises to the top of the brine. It will take 4 or 5 days until the pickles are half done. If this is the flavor you prefer, you can remove the pickles from the crock and place them in clean jars. Be sure to fill the jars with the pickling brine, some dill, and garlic cloves. Seal the jars tightly and refrigerate them. The cucumbers will continue to pickle, but much more slowly.

If you leave the pickles in the crock, they will be completely sour in about 10 days. Be sure to remove the pickles from the brine when they have reached the desired flavor. Place the pickles in a clean jar with brine, dill, and garlic from the pickling solution. Store in the refrigerator for up to 6 months.

*Hint*

You can also use this recipe to make pickled green tomatoes.

# SMOKED SALMON SPREAD

## Ingredients

½ pound smoked salmon

1 medium onion, finely
    chopped

1 teaspoon dried dill

½ cup sour cream, regular
    or fat-free

½ cup mayonnaise, regular
    or fat-free

Ground pepper to taste

*T*his is a great spread for bagels and makes a small amount of expensive, smoked salmon go a long way—with a lot less fat. You can use the end pieces of salmon if you can find them.

**Makes 2½ cups**

Use a food processor to blend all the ingredients. Chill thoroughly and serve.

This will keep refrigerated for several weeks. Serve with sliced bagels or rye bread.

# NACHOS

**Ingredients**

*U*se your imagination with this dish. It is a great snacking food and is easy to prepare. Add meat, different cheeses, and lots of salsa, then crunch away to your heart's desire.

**Serves 4 to 8**

1 bag (6 ounces) tortilla chips

8 ounces Monterey Jack cheese, grated (2 cups)

1 can (7 ounces) chopped green chiles

Place the chips on a large plate. Heat the cheese in the microwave or the top of a double boiler until melted and stir in the chiles.

Pour the hot cheese mixture over the tortilla chips and serve while the cheese is warm.

# EGGPLANT CAVIAR

## Ingredients

1 medium eggplant

1 medium onion, finely
  chopped

2 teaspoons chopped garlic

1 ripe tomato, peeled,
  seeded, and finely
  chopped

1 teaspoon sugar

3 tablespoons olive oil

2 tablespoons vinegar

Salt and pepper to taste

*T*his delicious spread or dip is low calorie. Often called "Cowboy Caviar" in gourmet shops, it is fabulous with crackers or served over a baked potato.

**Serves 8**

Slice the eggplant and broil the pieces until the skin is black and the pulp is very soft—about 10 minutes. Cool and finely chop. Mix the eggplant with the remaining ingredients. Cover and refrigerate for several hours or overnight so that the flavors marinate.

# CHEESE STICKS

These do require some work but they are comfort food prize winners and super with soup. These are just like the cheese sticks you can order from gourmet stores.

**Makes 36 cheese sticks**

Cream the butter and cheese. Add the milk and seasonings. Mix well.

Add the flour and bread crumbs and mix until well blended. Divide the dough into two parts and form into balls. Wrap in plastic wrap and refrigerate for at least 1 hour.

Preheat the oven to 350°F.

Roll each portion of the dough between 2 sheets of wax paper until they are about 1/8 inch thick.

Cut into strips 3/4 inch wide and 6 inches long. Sprinkle with coarse salt, Parmesan cheese, and sesame or poppy seeds.

Place the cheese sticks on an ungreased cookie sheet and bake for 12 to 15 minutes.

## Ingredients

4 tablespoons (1/2 stick) butter, at room temperature
4 ounces sharp Cheddar cheese, grated (1 cup)
1/4 cup milk
Pinch of salt
Dash of hot sauce
Pinch of paprika
Pinch of cayenne pepper
1/4 cup flour
1 1/2 cups dry bread crumbs
Coarse salt
Grated Parmesan cheese
Sesame or poppy seeds

# CHILE CON QUESO

## Ingredients

1 large onion, finely
    chopped
4 tablespoons (1/2 stick)
    butter
1 can (28 ounces) stewed
    tomatoes, drained and
    chopped
1 1/2 pounds sharp Cheddar
    cheese, grated (6 cups)
1 can (7 ounces) diced
    green chile peppers
Tabasco sauce to taste
Warm tortilla chips

*Chile con queso* means "chile peppers with cheese." Lots of people have told me that chips and dips are their idea of comfort foods. This snack is a step beyond the ordinary.

**Serves 12**

Sauté the onions in the butter until they are clear. Add the chopped tomatoes and simmer for 15 minutes or until the mixture becomes thick.

Add the cheese and stir until the cheese is melted. Add the chopped chiles. Season with Tabasco sauce.

Serve warm in a chafing dish. Scoop the dip with warm tortilla chips.

# CHEESE FONDUE

*C*lassic and classy comfort food. Here is the basic Swiss recipe. You will need a fondue pot and fondue forks, otherwise use the microwave and salad forks. You may need to reheat the fondue occasionally if you don't use a fondue pot. Be brave, experiment with different cheeses and eliminate the kirsch (cherry brandy) if you like. The alcohol in the wine will burn off, so you can serve this to kids.

**Serves 6**

Cut the bread into cubes making sure each piece has a crust. Allow the bread to dry out a little or crisp it for about 10 minutes in a 350°F oven. Toss the cheeses with the cornstarch until the cheese is coated.

Rub the inside of a 2-quart fondue pot with the garlic. Pour the wine and kirsch into the pot and cook over low heat for about 10 minutes. Make sure it does not boil, but that it is hot enough to melt the cheese.

Add the cheese mixture and stir until melted. Add the rest of the ingredients and stir until smooth.

Transfer to a fondue pot and serve hot, dipping in the bread cubes to your heart's content.

## Ingredients

1 loaf French bread, preferably a little stale
1/2 pound Emmentaler cheese, grated (2 cups)
1/2 pound Gruyère cheese, grated (2 cups)
2 tablespoons cornstarch
1 clove garlic
1 cup white wine
2 tablespoons kirsch
1 tablespoon lemon juice
Pinch of salt
Pinch of white pepper
Pinch of grated nutmeg

# SWISS FONDUE

## Ingredients

1 loaf French or Italian
   bread, preferably a little
   stale
1 clove garlic
2 tablespoons cornstarch
2 tablespoons cherry
   brandy (kirschwasser)
2 cups dry white wine
1 pound aged Swiss cheese,
   grated (4 cups)
White pepper, nutmeg, or
   paprika

*F*ondue can be served as an appetizer or as a main dish. It's very comforting to sit around the fondue pot and dip chunks of French bread into the fondue, drink wine, and gossip. You can experiment with different cheeses and eliminate the wine or the brandy or both and still have fun with this dish.

**Serves 4**

Cut the bread into cubes making sure each piece has a crust. Allow the bread to dry out a little or crisp it for about 10 minutes in a 350°F oven.

Rub the inside of a 2-quart fondue pot with garlic. In a small bowl, mix the cornstarch with the cherry brandy and set aside. You can replace the cherry brandy with 2 tablespoons of wine.

Heat the wine in an uncovered pot over low heat. When it starts to bubble, add the cheese slowly and cook, stirring constantly until the cheese melts. Add the cornstarch mixture and stir until the fondue thickens. Add seasonings to taste.

Transfer to a fondue pot and serve hot, using the bread chunks for dipping.

# ITALIAN FONDUE

*A* variation of the all-cheese fondue.

Serves 4

Rub the inside of a 2-quart fondue pot with the garlic. In a saucepan, brown the ground beef and stir in the tomato paste and cornstarch. Heat until warm. Transfer to the fondue pot and keep warm over low heat.

Stir in the cheeses, a little at a time, until they start to melt. Add the wine and stir until the mixture is well blended.

Add the seasonings and serve hot, scooping the sauce with the chunks of bread.

## Ingredients

1 clove garlic

½ pound ground beef

1 can (15 ounces) tomato paste

1 tablespoon cornstarch

1 pound mozzarella cheese, grated (4 cups)

1 container (8 ounces) cottage cheese

½ cup dry wine

1 teaspoon salt

1 teaspoon oregano

¼ teaspoon ground pepper

1 loaf French bread, cut into chunks

# SEAFOOD FONDUE

## Ingredients

1 can (13 ounces) crab,
    lobster, or shrimp bisque
2 tablespoons butter
1/4 teaspoon dry dill
1/2 pound aged Swiss
    cheese, grated (2 cups)
1/2 teaspoon salt
1/4 teaspoon dry mustard
1/4 teaspoon pepper
32 large shrimp, cooked
    and cleaned
1 loaf French bread, cut
    into chunks

*A*nother version of fondue to keep your fondue fork and pot in motion. This is great!

**Serves 4**

Heat the bisque with the butter and dill in a fondue pot over medium heat. When thoroughly heated, slowly stir in the cheese. *Do not boil.* Stir in the seasonings until mixture is well blended.

Spear shrimp and bread chunks with fondue forks and dip into the fondue.

# CHOPPED LIVER

*T*he fancy name for this is "liver pâté" and there are people who would kill for this delicacy. This is the basic recipe to which you may add brandy, chopped nuts, or whatever you like.

**Makes 3 cups**

Melt the chicken fat in a frying pan and cook the onions until they are transparent. Add the chicken livers and sauté until they are browned. Don't overcook the livers or they will not be tender.

In a food processor, blend the onions, liver, and eggs. If you prefer a coarser version, use a meat grinder. Add the seasonings and mix well.

Refrigerate. Serve with a bowl of fresh vegetables and crackers.

## Ingredients

1/4 cup rendered chicken
 fat *or* 4 tablespoons
 (1/2 stick) butter
2 large onions, thinly sliced
1 pound chicken livers,
 rinsed and drained
4 hard boiled eggs
1 teaspoon salt
1/4 teaspoon ground pepper
Pinch of garlic powder

# STUFFED MUSHROOMS

## Ingredients

1 pound large mushrooms
2 tablespoons (1/4 stick) butter
1 package (3 ounces) cream cheese
2 tablespoons chopped onion
1/2 teaspoon herbs
Paprika

*T*hese are easier to make than you would think and very impressive to serve. You can use any herbs you like. I prefer a combination of parsley, chives, salt, and white pepper.

**Serves 8**

Preheat the broiler. Wash the mushrooms and remove the stems. Finely chop the stems.

Melt the butter in a large pan. Brown the mushroom caps, round side down, in the butter for 2 minutes. Remove from the heat and drain on paper towels.

In another bowl, combine the cream cheese, onion, chopped mushroom stems, and the herbs and stuff the mixture into the mushroom caps. Dust lightly with paprika.

Broil the mushroom caps until the cheese mixture is bubbly.

## Hint

You can add 1/4 cup seasoned bread crumbs, finely chopped pieces of chicken or sausage, or whatever you desire to the basic cheese mixture.

# ONION TOAST

*T*his toast is terrific with a bowl of hot soup—perfect comfort food. If onions aren't your thing, try garlic or Parmesan cheese. This is fast and easy to prepare.

**Serves 8**

Mix the mayonnaise and the chopped onion. Add salt and pepper to taste.

Spread the mixture on top of the bread and broil the bread until it becomes bubbly and brown. Serve hot.

## Ingredients

3 tablespoons mayonnaise
1 sweet onion, finely chopped
Salt and ground black pepper
8 slices of French bread, cut in half

# CAVIAR HORS D'OEUVRES

## Ingredients

12 eggs at room
    temperature
1/4 cup finely chopped
    green onion
1/4 cup mayonnaise
1/2 teaspoon salt
1/4 teaspoon ground pepper
1/4 teaspoon dry mustard
8 ounces caviar
1 cup sour cream
Sprigs of parsley for garnish

*I* consider fine caviar the adult version of candy snaps. I prefer the expensive kind but I'll settle for any kind I can get. It's the saltiness that makes caviar a comfort food for me. This appetizer can be prepared the day before serving.

**Serves 10 generously**

To boil the eggs, place them in the bottom of a large pot and cover them with water. Bring the water to a boil and then turn off the heat and cover the pot. The eggs will be perfect after 20 minutes. Drain the water and cover the eggs with cold water and ice cubes.

Chop the eggs coarsely and combine with the onion, mayonnaise, salt, pepper, and mustard. Use more mayonnaise if necessary.

Spoon the egg salad into a large glass bowl. Spread the egg salad smooth and cover with the caviar. Spoon the sour cream over the caviar and refrigerate the salad for up to 24 hours before serving.

Decorate with sprigs of parsley and let your guests spoon the caviar, eggs, and sour cream onto melba toast or bread.

# DEEP-FRIED CHEESE

*A*nything that is deep-fried is my idea of a comfort food. Give me fried Camembert or Brie cheese, and I am in heaven.

**Makes 8 squares of fried cheese**

Cut the cheese into 2 × 2-inch squares. Roll the cheese in the flour and shake off the excess.

Using a fondue fork or tongs, dip the cheese into the egg and then roll the cheese in the bread crumbs. Make sure the cheese is completely coated.

Heat oil in a deep fryer or a frying pan to 350°F. Fry the cheese in oil for a minute or two, until it is golden brown. Drain on paper towels.

## Ingredients

8 ounces chilled Brie, Camembert, or Cheddar cheese
2 tablespoons flour
1 egg, well beaten
1 cup dry bread crumbs
Oil for frying

## Hint

Double the recipe if you are serving more than yourself!

# EGGPLANT FRITTERS

## Ingredients

1 large eggplant
1 tablespoon salt
1⅓ cups flour
1 cup club soda
2 tablespoons oil
2 egg whites
Oil for deep-frying

*C*runchy, delicately flavored, nutty, and sweet eggplant makes a fabulous fritter. You can use any of the marvelous eggplants available or zucchini.

**Serves 6**

Cut the eggplant into finger-size pieces. Place in a colander, sprinkle with 1 tablespoon salt, and let the eggplant drain for an hour or two.

Combine 1 cup flour, pinch of salt, club soda, and 2 tablespoons oil. Cover the mixture, and let it stand for an hour at room temperature.

Pat the eggplant dry using paper towels. Place ⅓ cup flour in a bag with the eggplant chunks and shake until the eggplant is well coated.

In a deep fryer or a frying pan, heat the oil to 350°F.

Beat the egg whites until they are stiff and fold them into the batter. If necessary, add a bit more club soda. Dip the eggplant pieces into the batter, one at a time.

Fry the eggplant in the hot oil until golden brown. Drain on paper towels and serve warm to thunderous applause.

# ARTICHOKE DIP

*T*he first time I tasted this wonderful dip, I begged for the recipe. It's really very simple. The hardest part is waiting for the finished dip to come out of the oven.

**Makes 3 cups**

## Ingredients

1 can (14 ounces) artichoke hearts (not marinated), drained

3/4 cup mayonnaise

1 cup freshly grated Parmesan cheese

1 teaspoon minced garlic

1/4 teaspoon Worcestershire sauce

Few drops of hot sauce

Preheat the oven to 350°F.

Combine all the ingredients and spoon into a lightly buttered 4-cup casserole. Bake for 20 minutes or until hot and bubbly. Serve with crackers or toast thins.

# BAKED BRIE

## Ingredients

1 (8-ounce) Brie or Gouda
   cheese

1 package (8 ounces) refrigerated crescent rolls

1 egg, beaten with 2 tablespoons water

*T*his is one of the most elegant and simple appetizers you can serve and a real comfort food.

**Serves 4**

Preheat the oven to 400°F.

Remove the wax seal from around the cheese and freeze it for one hour. Remove the crescent rolls from the package, unroll, and press dough together into one large round. Place the frozen cheese in the center of the dough and wrap the cheese completely. Brush the egg mixture over the pastry.

Bake for 20 minutes or until the pastry is golden brown. Serve hot or cold in slices.

# MUSHROOMS STUFFED WITH CHEESE

What a tempting appetizer to warm your guests. You can add chopped crab or cooked chopped sausage. These are always wonderful.

**Serves 12**

Preheat the oven to 350°F.

Remove the stems from the mushrooms and set the caps aside. Chop the stems and add all the remaining ingredients except for the olive oil. Mix well. Press enough of this mixture into each mushroom cap so that the filling is slightly mounded over the cap.

Spread a little olive oil evenly on a baking dish. Put the mushrooms, filling side up, into the baking dish so that they do not overlap.

Drizzle the remaining olive oil over the mushrooms.

Bake for 30 minutes or until the tops of the mushrooms are golden brown.

## Ingredients

2 pounds large mushrooms

1/2 cup grated Parmesan cheese

3/4 cup dry bread crumbs

1/2 cup grated onion

1 teaspoon minced garlic

3 tablespoons minced parsley

1 teaspoon salt

1/2 teaspoon pepper

1/2 cup olive oil

# MERRILL'S MEATBALLS

## Ingredients

2 pounds lean ground beef

¼ cup water

1 small onion, grated

2 eggs, beaten

1 cup cracker crumbs or
bread crumbs

1 teaspoon salt

1 can (1 pound) jellied
cranberry sauce

1 bottle (12 ounces) chili
sauce

2 tablespoons brown sugar

1 tablespoon lemon juice

*T*his recipe is from my darling Texas friend, Merrill Lipowsky. I have been making similar meatballs for years and everyone loves them.

**Serves 8**

Combine the meat with the water, onion, eggs, crumbs, and salt and shape the mixture into bite-size meatballs.

In a large saucepan combine the cranberry sauce, chili sauce, brown sugar, and lemon juice. Heat and stir until smooth.

Add the uncooked meatballs to the sauce, cover, and simmer for 1 hour. Skim off the fat and serve the meatballs in a fondue pot with fancy toothpicks.

# CRAB CANAPÉS

*P*op these canapés out of the freezer and under the broiler and listen to the compliments. Perfect for those unexpected guests.

**Makes 48 canapés**

Mix all the ingredients except for the muffins until smooth. Spread on muffin halves and cut into quarters. Freeze for at least one hour and then broil until they puff up and are golden brown, about 10 minutes.

## Ingredients

1 can (7 ounces) crab meat
   or ½ pound fresh
½ cup (1 stick) butter
1 jar (7 ounces) sharp
   Cheddar cheese spread
2 tablespoons mayonnaise
½ teaspoon seasoned salt
½ teaspoon garlic powder
6 English muffins, split into
   halves

# CRAB CAKES

## Ingredients

2 eggs, slightly beaten

2 tablespoons mayonnaise

1 teaspoon prepared
   mustard

2 slices day-old bread, with
   the crusts removed

1 teaspoon Worcestershire
   sauce

½ teaspoon salt

½ teaspoon pepper

1 pound crab meat

Oil or butter for frying

*T*hese can be served as an appetizer or as an entrée. They are wonderful either way.

**Serves 4 as an entrée, 8 as appetizers**

Mix all the ingredients except for the crab and oil. Add the crab meat and mix gently. Shape into patties and refrigerate for at least 1 hour in order to make them easier to fry.

Heat oil in a large frying pan. Fry the crab cakes in the oil until they are browned and crisp on both sides.

# BEAN DIP

*N*o party is complete without bean dip served with a big bowl of crunchy tortilla chips. Olé!

**Makes 2 cups dip**

Cream the cheese and add the refried beans. Add the remaining ingredients, blending well. Refrigerate for a few hours and serve with warm tortilla chips.

## Ingredients

1 package (3 ounces) cream cheese, at room temperature

1 can (8 ounces) refried beans

1/2 cup sour cream

1 tablespoon minced onion

1 teaspoon minced garlic

2 teaspoons diced green chiles

2 teaspoons bottled chili sauce

1 teaspoon chili powder

1/2 teaspoon Worcestershire sauce

# SEAFOOD COCKTAILS

**Cocktail sauce**

1 cup bottled chili sauce

3 tablespoons lemon juice

1 tablespoon prepared
    horseradish

1/2 teaspoon grated onion

Few drops of hot pepper
    sauce

*M*ake sure that the seafood is cold and crisp before you serve it.

**Makes 1 1/2 cups cocktail sauce**

Combine the sauce ingredients and mix well. Chill and serve with seafood cocktails.

*For shrimp cocktail:* Allow 6 to 8 medium shrimp or 3 ounces of the tiny salad shrimp per person. Cook and devein shrimp. Chill and serve on shredded lettuce in chilled cocktail cups with cocktail sauce.

*For crab cocktail:* Flake 1 cup fresh crab or 1 can (7 ounces) of crab meat. Mix with 1 cup finely chopped celery and chill. Serve in cocktail glasses, over shredded lettuce, with cocktail sauce.

# NIBBLE MIX

---

**T**his mix is addictive! This recipe makes enough so that you can binge and store the remainder in a can with a tight-fitting lid for snacks.

**Makes 2 quarts**

Preheat the oven to 250°F.

Mix all the ingredients and pour onto 2 large baking pans. Bake for 2 hours, stirring every 15 minutes.

## Ingredients

2 pounds salted nuts, mixed

1 package (11 ounces) spoon-size shredded wheat

1 package (10½ ounces) doughnut-shaped oat cereal

1 package (6 ounces) crisp rice squares cereal

1 package (7 ounces) small pretzel twists

1 bag (5¾ ounces) pretzel sticks

1 bag (4½ ounces) pretzel bits

2 cups salad oil

1 tablespoon garlic powder

1 tablespoon seasoned salt

## Hint

This mix is less expensive to make than it is to buy it already prepared in little cellophane bags. Feel free to add additional goodies to the mix.

# CHINESE POTSTICKERS

## Ingredients

1½ pounds ground pork

⅓ cup soy sauce

6 green onions, minced

4 ounces salad shrimp

1 tablespoon peanut oil

½ teaspoon grated ginger

1 egg

2 cloves garlic, minced

1 pound Chinese cabbage

2 teaspoons salt

1 package wonton wrappers

2 teaspoons peanut oil for
    frying

*I*n San Francisco there are dim sum parlors the size of a football field. Waitresses swirl by pushing carts with various potstickers in bowls. You can eat as much as you like and pay for each bowl separately. I ended up with boiled chicken feet on one occasion, which I definitely did not consider to be comfort food.

Buy the prepared wonton wrappers in the produce department of your supermarket and follow the package directions for rolling the wontons.

**Makes 60**

Combine all the ingredients except for the cabbage, salt, wrappers, and frying oil. Mix well and set aside.

Core the cabbage and chop it finely. Cover the cabbage with salt and let it sit for at least 1 hour. Press out the water from the cabbage and mix the cabbage into the meat mixture.

*Assembling the potstickers:* Lay out the wonton wrappers on a large flat surface. Place 1 teaspoon of meat filling in the center of each wonton wrapper and fold each potsticker so that it resembles a triangle. Pinch the edges together to seal. Use a little water on the edges of the wonton to help seal it shut.

Heat 2 teaspoons of peanut oil in a skillet and stand the potstickers close together with the seam-side up. Sauté over medium heat for a few minutes but don't let them burn.

Add ½ cup water, cover, and steam for 20 minutes. Serve immediately with vinegar, soy sauce, or Chinese hot oil.

*Hint*

These can be used as appetizers or for a dinner entrée.

# BREADS

*B*read is a great comfort food. To me, the smell of freshly baked bread is better than the most expensive perfume. When I was a Realtor and had open houses for sale, I would often defrost a loaf of commercial frozen bread and bake it in the house I was showing because it made the house feel like home.

The following recipes are practically guaranteed to make you an unforgettable baker.

# SOPAIPILLA MEXICAN FRIED BREAD

*Ingredients*

4 tablespoons lard
4 cups flour
1 teaspoon salt
2 teaspoons baking powder
4 eggs
1 cup sugar
Water or milk
1 teaspoon cinnamon mixed
    with ½ cup sugar
Sugar

*I* love fried foods and Mexican foods—not necessarily in that order. I first tasted these puffy pastries in New Mexico and knew I was hooked. You can use vegetable shortening to make these if lard is offensive to you, but somehow they are not nearly as delicious.

They need to be fried and eaten immediately. You can sprinkle a little cinnamon-sugar on the tops and eat them right out of the fryer.

**Makes 36 sopaipillas**

Mix together the lard, flour, salt, and baking powder until crumbly. Add the eggs, sugar, and enough water or milk to make a medium dough. Knead for a few turns, cover, and let the dough rest for 30 minutes.

Roll the dough into a rectangle ¼ inch thick and cut into wedges. Fry in hot oil, turning each sopaipilla once to brown on both sides.

Sprinkle the cinnamon and sugar on the hot sopaipillas or serve them plain.

# FUDGE WAFFLES

## Ingredients

2 ounces unsweetened
   chocolate

4 tablespoons (1/2 stick)
   butter

3 eggs

2/3 cup sugar

1 teaspoon vanilla

1 cup buttermilk

1 1/4 cup flour

1/2 teaspoon baking soda

1/2 teaspoon baking powder

Pinch of salt

3 ounces semisweet
   chocolate, chopped

*T*he ultimate in satisfaction for the waffle lover. Serve these hot with whipped cream, strawberries, and fudge sauce.

**Makes 6 waffles**

Prepare the waffle maker according to the manufacturer's directions. Melt the unsweetened chocolate and butter together in the microwave on high for 1 minute, and stir until smooth. Cool the mixture.

In a large bowl, beat the eggs, sugar, and vanilla together and blend in the buttermilk. Stir in the melted chocolate mixture. Add the flour, baking soda, baking powder, and salt and stir until smooth. Fold in the chopped chocolate and bake in the prepared waffle maker.

# SOUR CREAM WAFFLES

*H*ow wonderful to wake up to the smell of waffles being baked. Smother the waffles with fresh sliced strawberries and whipping cream for a heavenly treat.

**Makes 6 waffles**

Preheat the waffle maker. Sift the flour and add sugar, baking powder, baking soda, and salt.

Use an electric mixer to beat the eggs until they are thick and lemon colored. Blend in the sour cream. Add the dry ingredients and the melted butter and blend until well mixed.

Bake according to the manufacturer's instructions.

## Ingredients

1 1/2 cups flour

1 teaspoon sugar

1/4 teaspoon baking soda

1/2 teaspoon baking powder

1/2 teaspoon salt

3 eggs

2 cups (1 pint) sour cream

4 tablespoons (1/2 stick)
   butter, melted

# BAKED BANANA PANCKAES

## Ingredients

¹⁄₂ cup (1 stick) butter

6 eggs, at room temperature

1 cup milk

¹⁄₄ cup plus 2 tablespoons orange liqueur or orange juice

1 cup flour

¹⁄₂ cup sugar

Pinch of salt

2 bananas, cut into thin slices, *or* 1 basket fresh strawberries, sliced

Powdered sugar, optional

*7*hese pancakes are certifiable comfort foods. You can replace the bananas with fresh strawberries.

**Serves 4**

Preheat the oven to 425°F. Don't forget it takes 10 minutes for your oven to reach the desired temperature.

Place the butter into a 9 × 13-inch baking pan and place it in the oven until the butter melts and is bubbling.

Mix together the eggs, milk, ¹⁄₄ cup orange liqueur, flour, sugar, and salt until well blended. Pour the batter over the melted butter in the pan and bake for 10 minutes until the pancake has started to puff.

While the pancake is baking, heat the bananas or strawberries in a saucepan together with a pinch of sugar and the remaining 2 tablespoons of orange liqueur.

Allow the pancake to continue baking until it is very puffy and golden brown. Pour the bananas or strawberries over the pancake and serve immediately. If you prefer, you can dust powdered sugar over the pancake.

# SWEDISH PANCAKES
# WITH BANANAS

## Ingredients

1 cup cottage cheese
3 tablespoons honey
1 cup sour cream
1 teaspoon vanilla
Pinch of salt
4 eggs, at room
    temperature
1 cup flour
1 teaspoon baking powder
2 bananas, cut into 1/4-inch
    diagonal slices
Flour
Vegetable oil or butter

*7*he batter for these pancakes can be whipped up in your blender or food processor. Everyone will want seconds.

Serves 4

Blend the cottage cheese, honey, sour cream, vanilla, and salt together in the food processor until very smooth. Add the eggs, one at a time. Sift the flour and baking powder into a bowl and slowly add the egg mixture. Do not overmix.

Lightly dust the sliced bananas with flour. Heat a griddle or large frying pan and brush butter or oil onto the surface of the pan. Drop the batter by the tablespoonful onto the heated pan and top each pancake with a slice of banana. Spoon another tablespoonful of batter on top of the sliced banana. Cook until golden brown. Turn each pancake and continue to cook until golden.

Serve with warm maple syrup.

# CURRANT SCONES

## Ingredients

2 cups flour

1/4 cup sugar

2 teaspoons baking powder

1/3 cup butter, chilled and
cut into small pieces

1/2 cup heavy cream

1 egg

1 tablespoon vanilla or
lemon extract

1/2 cup currants

### Glaze

1 egg

1 teaspoon water

Scones are another comfort food. They need to be baked and eaten as soon as possible after being removed from the oven because they become increasingly dry with each passing moment. One famous mix contains only the flour and baking powder and sells for $5 a bag. Make your own instead!

You can replace the currants, which are really tiny raisins, with raisins, dates, chopped prunes, or figs. I use dried blueberries and they are marvelous. I first soak dried fruit in very hot water for 15 minutes to puff it up. Then I drain the fruit and add it to the batter.

Serves 8

Preheat the oven to 425°F.

Lightly oil a cookie sheet or cover it with parchment paper. Stir together the flour, sugar, and baking powder. Cut the butter into the dry ingredients using a food processor with a metal blade. The butter-flour mixture will resemble small beans. Add the heavy cream, egg, and vanilla. Add the currants.

Form the dough into a ball and work the dough with your fingers until it is relatively smooth and no longer crumbly. Shape the dough into a circle about 8 inches across on the cookie sheet. You can use your fingers to pat out the dough if you don't want to roll it out.

Score the dough into 12 wedges. Mix the glaze ingredients together and brush over the dough. Bake for 12 to 15 minutes or until golden brown. Using a sharp knife, cut through the markings and serve as individual scones.

# FRENCH TOAST SOUFFLÉ

## Ingredients

1 loaf challah bread, cut
    into thick slices
1/2 cup (1 stick) butter,
    melted
4 large eggs
1/4 cup sugar
2 cups cream or
    half-and-half
1 teaspoon cinnamon
1 teaspoon vanilla
Maple syrup, jam, or jelly
    for topping

*T*his is fabulously delicious and can make you famous for your brunches. You can buy the egg bread known as challah or make your own (page 50). It's even better if the bread is stale.

This can be partially prepared the night before and kept refrigerated until morning. Put it in the oven before your shower and it will be ready to serve when the coffee is brewed.

**Serves 8**

Butter a large baking dish pretty enough to use for serving. Place the sliced challah into the baking dish. Pour the melted butter over the bread.

Mix together the eggs and sugar. Add the cream, cinnamon, and vanilla. Pour it over the bread and let it soak for at least an hour or keep refrigerated overnight. Use a pancake turner to turn the slices very carefully once or twice to make sure the bread is saturated. Try not to break the bread—it will still be delicious, but not quite as pretty.

Preheat the oven to 350°F. If the bread has been refrigerated overnight, remove it from the refrigerator and let it come to room temperature while the oven is heating.

Sprinkle additional cinnamon and sugar on top of the bread and bake uncovered for 45 minutes or until the bread is puffy and golden brown. Serve hot with the topping of your choice.

# DILLY CASSEROLE BREAD

This recipe is from Betty Ann Osborne and is one of the most flavorful breads I've ever tasted.

**Makes 1 round loaf; serves 8**

Sprinkle the dry yeast over the warm water (110° to 115°F) or crumble the yeast cake into warm water (110°F). Heat the cottage cheese to lukewarm and combine with the sugar, onion, butter, dill, salt, baking soda, egg, and yeast mixture.

Add enough flour to form a soft dough, beating well after each addition. Cover and let the dough rest in a warm place until it is doubled, about 1 hour. Punch the dough down and turn it into a greased 6-cup baking pan. Let the dough rest for an additional 30 to 40 minutes.

Preheat the oven to 350°F. Don't forget it takes 10 minutes for the oven to heat to your desired temperature

Bake for 40 to 50 minutes or until the bread is golden brown. If desired, brush the top of the bread with additional butter and sprinkle with a little salt immediately after baking.

## Ingredients

1 package (¼ ounce) dry yeast or 1 yeast cake
¼ cup warm water
1 cup creamed cottage cheese
2 tablespoons sugar
1 tablespoon instant minced onion
1 tablespoon butter
2 tablespoons dill weed
1 teaspoon salt
¼ teaspoon baking soda
1 egg
2¼ to 2½ cups flour

# BUTTERMILK BISCUITS

## Ingredients

3 cups flour

1 tablespoon baking
    powder

1 tablespoon baking soda

3/4 cup (1 1/2 sticks) butter, at
    room temperature

1 1/2 cups buttermilk

*T*hese are the old-fashioned, down-home kind of biscuits that go with simmering soups and savory stews. They are wonderful plain or with butter, cream cheese, or honey.

**Makes 1 dozen**

Preheat the oven to 425°F.

Combine the dry ingredients and cut the butter into the flour mixture. Stir just enough milk to blend. Roll the dough on a floured board to a thickness of 1/2 inch. Cut the dough into rounds with a biscuit cutter or a glass that is 3 inches across.

Place the biscuits on a lightly greased cookie sheet and bake for 15 minutes or until the biscuits are golden brown.

## Hint

If you want to make cheese biscuits, add 1 1/2 cups of grated sharp Cheddar cheese to the batter before rolling out the dough.

# FOCACCIA (ITALIAN FLATBREAD)

*I* first tasted focaccia in New York. What bliss! You can add sun-dried tomatoes, garlic, minced onion, or cheese. It's wonderful served with hot soup and savory stews. My friend Susan Morton, who is Italian, says it is pronounced fo-GOT-sha.

**Serves 12**

Dissolve the yeast in ¼ cup of the warm water (110° to 115°F) and set it aside until it becomes bubbly. Mix together the flour, olive oil, and 4 teaspoons salt. Add the yeast mixture and the remaining 2½ cups water. Knead the dough by hand until it is smooth and elastic. Place the dough in a large greased bowl, cover, and set it in a warm place. Allow the dough to rise until it has doubled, 1 to 2 hours.

Preheat the oven to 400°F. Punch down the dough. Place the dough onto a large cookie sheet that has been lightly coated with oil. Flatten the dough to a thickness of ¼ inch. Make indentations all over the dough with your thumbs. Brush the top with olive oil and sprinkle with the kosher salt.

Bake for 25 minutes or until golden brown.

## Ingredients

2 packages (¼ ounce each) dry yeast

2¾ cups warm water

8 cups flour

2 tablespoons olive oil

4 teaspoons salt

Olive oil

Coarse kosher salt

## Hint

Press sun-dried tomatoes, cheese, and minced garlic or onion into the dough before baking.

# EGG BAGELS

## Ingredients

2 packages (¼ ounce each)
   dry yeast
¼ cup sugar
2 teaspoons salt
½ cup hot water
   (110° to 115°F)
½ cup oil
3 eggs
5 to 6 cups flour
¼ cup water

**Toppings (optional)**

Poppy seeds
Sesame seeds
Garlic
Chopped onion

*B*agels are as much fun to make as they are to eat. You can use lots of different toppings: fried onion bits, sesame seeds, garlic, or poppy seeds. You can add raisins and cinnamon to the batter.

**Makes 18 bagels**

Mix the yeast, sugar, and salt in a bowl and add the hot water. Stir until the yeast is dissolved. Blend in the oil and 2 eggs and add enough flour to make a stiff dough.

Knead the dough on a floured surface until it becomes elastic and smooth, 2 to 3 minutes.

Place the dough in a greased bowl and turn the dough to grease all over. Cover the dough and allow it to double in size—about 1 hour.

Punch down the dough and knead it. Divide it into 18 pieces and roll out each piece into a log about 10 inches long. Pinch the edges together to make a circle.

Preheat the broiler. Place the bagels on a cookie sheet. Mix 1 egg with ¼ cup water and brush it on the tops of the bagels. Sprinkle each bagel with topping of your choice. Broil the bagels for 2 minutes on each side or until the bagels turn golden.

Preheat the oven to 350°F.

Boil 2 quarts of water and drop the bagels, one at a time, into the boiling water. Simmer for 5 minutes. Drain the bagels and place them on greased cookie sheets. Bake for 35 to 40 minutes or until the bagels are brown. Serve the bagels warm or toasted.

Cool and slice any bagels that you don't use the same day and freeze them.

# CHALLAH

## Ingredients

2 packages (¼ ounce each)
    dry yeast

⅔ cup warm water (110°
    to 115°F)

6 egg yolks

3 whole eggs

½ cup vegetable oil

¼ cup sugar

1 teaspoon salt

4½ cups flour

1 egg, beaten with a pinch
    of salt

*C*hallah is a rich and delicious egg bread. It can be shaped several different ways. It can be formed into three long ropes and then braided together; formed into one long rope and then wound together like a snake; or baked in one round loaf. The leftovers are fabulous for French toast, bread pudding, or for dipping in fondue.

**Makes 1 loaf**

In a large bowl, dissolve the yeast in the warm water and stir in the egg yolks, 3 whole eggs, oil, sugar, and salt. Add enough flour to make a sticky dough.

Knead the dough on a floured surface until it is smooth and elastic, about 5 minutes.

Place the dough into a greased bowl and turn it so that it is coated all over with the grease. Place the dough, covered, in a draft-free area and allow it to rise until double in size, about 2 hours.

Punch down the dough and divide it into three pieces. Roll each piece into a roll about 12 inches long. Braid the three pieces together and pinch the ends to seal them.

Place the challah on a greased cookie sheet. Brush the bread with egg-salt mixture. Let the bread rise until it has doubled in size—about 45 minutes. Brush the bread again with the egg mixture.

Preheat the oven to 375°F and bake for 40 minutes or until the bread is golden brown.

## Hint

For raisin challah, soak 1 cup of raisins in hot water for 15 minutes and drain. Add raisins to the dough before letting the dough rise the first time.

# CORN MUFFINS

## Ingredients

1 cup yellow cornmeal
1 cup flour
1/4 cup sugar
4 teaspoons baking powder
1/2 teaspoon salt
1 egg
1 cup milk
1/4 cup vegetable oil
1/2 teaspoon lemon juice or
    flavoring
1/2 teaspoon vanilla

## Hint

Poke tiny holes in the
baked corn muffins and
pour 4 tablespoons (1/2
stick) of melted butter onto
the cornbread before
serving.

*S*erve these muffins hot, right out of the oven.
Perfect with chili, stew, or even breakfast.

**Makes 12 muffins**

Preheat the oven to 400°F.

Combine the cornmeal, flour, sugar, baking
powder, and salt. Add the remaining ingredients
and blend until smooth.

Fill a 12-cup muffin pan with paper liners and
fill the cups 2/3 full of batter.

Bake for 25 minutes or until the muffins are
golden brown. Serve warm.

# CORNBREAD

Cornbread should be served hot from the oven. I've added jalapeño peppers and Cheddar cheese to make this cornbread especially delicious.

**Serves 9**

Preheat the oven to 400°F. Butter a square 8 × 8-inch baking pan.

Sauté the onion in butter until the onion is almost transparent. Stir in the cheese until it melts. Add the sour cream and the peppers and set the mixture aside.

Mix together the flour, sugar, baking powder, salt, and cornmeal. Make a well in the center of these ingredients and add the eggs, milk, and melted butter. Mix until the ingredients are just combined and the batter is lumpy. Pour the batter into the prepared pan and sprinkle the onion mixture over the top. Swirl the onion mixture into the batter using a knife.

Bake for 20 minutes until cornbread is golden brown. Cut into slices and serve hot.

## Ingredients

1 medium onion, finely chopped

3 tablespoons butter

4 ounces Cheddar cheese, grated (1 cup)

1/2 cup sour cream

1 can (7 ounces) diced jalapeño peppers, drained

1 cup flour

2 tablespoons sugar

4 tablespoons baking powder

1/4 teaspoon salt

1 cup yellow cornmeal

2 eggs

1 cup milk

4 tablespoons (1/2 stick) butter, melted

## Hint

Poke holes all over the baked cornbread and pour 4 tablespoons (1/2 stick) melted butter over the cornbread before serving.

# MARVELOUS MUFFINS

## Ingredients

²/₃ cup raisins

2¹/₂ cups flour

³/₄ cup sugar

¹/₄ cup firmly packed brown
   sugar

2 teaspoons baking soda

2 teaspoons cinnamon

¹/₂ teaspoon salt

2 cups grated carrots

1 large tart apple, grated

¹/₂ cup any chopped nuts

¹/₃ cup flaked coconut

1 cup vegetable oil

4 eggs

2 teaspoons vanilla

¹/₂ teaspoon lemon juice

## Hint

For giant muffins, I save
tuna fish cans, run them
through the dishwasher, and
line them with extra-large,
store-bought paper cups. Put
the tins on a cookie sheet
and bake them as directed.

*7*hese make a delicious breakfast or brunch
treat. Serve with fresh fruit and coffee. Almost
everyone thinks of these as real comfort food.
You can make the batter the night before, preheat the oven when you awake, and have them
baked in time for breakfast.

**Makes 18 regular or 12 giant muffins**

Preheat the oven to 350°F. Line 18 regular or
12 giant muffin tins with baking cups.

Soak raisins in hot water until they plump.
Drain and set aside. Mix together the flour,
sugar, baking soda, cinnamon, and salt. Stir in
the raisins, carrots, apple, nuts, and coconut.

Beat the oil together with the eggs, vanilla,
and lemon juice and blend lightly into the flour
mixture.

Fill the cups ²/₃ full of batter and bake for 20
to 25 minutes (regular-size muffins) or 30 to 40
minutes (giant-size muffins) or until a tester inserted in the center of a muffin comes clean.

# BLUEBERRY MUFFINS

*W*hat pleasure it is to bite into a warm blueberry muffin. This is another recipe you can fix the night before and bake in the morning. If you want the batter to remain a light color, place the blueberries in a plastic bag with ½ cup flour. Shake and coat the berries and add them to the batter just before baking the muffins.

**Makes 24 muffins**

Preheat the oven to 400°F. Line 24 muffin tins with paper baking cups.

Blend together the eggs, milk, sugar, oil, and vanilla. Add flour, baking powder, and salt and fold in the blueberries.

Fill the muffin cups ⅔ full of batter and bake for 20 minutes or until the muffins are golden brown. Sprinkle with powdered sugar and serve warm.

## Ingredients

2 eggs
2 cups milk
1 cup sugar
2 cups vegetable oil
1 teaspoon vanilla
4 cups flour
6 teaspoons baking powder
1 teaspoon salt
2 cups fresh or 1 can
    (22 ounces) blueberries,
    drained

# CHOCOLATE PECAN MUFFINS

## Ingredients

6 ounces semisweet
  chocolate, chopped

3 tablespoons butter

1 cup flour

2 tablespoons sugar

2 teaspoons baking powder

1/2 teaspoon cinnamon

1 egg

1/3 cup buttermilk

1 teaspoon vanilla

3/4 cup chopped pecans

1 cup semisweet chocolate
  chips

### Topping (optional)

1/2 cup flour

1/4 cup firmly packed brown
  sugar

1/2 teaspoon cinnamon

2 tablespoons (1/4 stick)
  butter, melted

1/4 cup chopped pecans

*T*hese were my favorites at our bakery and dessert parlor. They are very moist, heavy, and yummy.

**Makes 12 muffins**

Preheat the oven to 375°F. Line a 12-cup muffin tin with paper cups.

Melt the 6 ounces of chopped semisweet chocolate and butter together in the microwave on high for 1 to 2 minutes and stir until smooth. Combine the flour, sugar, baking powder, and cinnamon. Mix well and add the egg, buttermilk, vanilla, and chocolate mixture. Stir to moisten and add the chopped pecans and the chocolate chips.

If you have time and want very special muffins, mix together the ingredients for the topping and sprinkle it on the tops of the muffins before baking them. Fill the muffin cups ³/₄ full and bake the muffins for 20 to 25 minutes or until a tester inserted in the center of a muffin comes clean.

## Hint

Double this recipe to make 12 giant muffins. Save tuna fish cans, run them through the dishwasher, and line them with extra-large, store-bought paper cups. Put the tins on a cookie sheet, fill them ³/₄ full, and bake them for 30 to 40 minutes.

# SOUPS

---

$S$oup is definitely comfort food, served cold or hot right out of the pot. Most people want their soup served in big bowls with crusty bread on the side to soak up the last drops on the bottom of the bowl.

Make a double recipe of your favorite soup and freeze half of it to take to an ailing friend or save it for a cold night or when you are in need of comforting.

# GUMBO

Make this with chicken, crab, shrimp, or a combination of all of these. This is wonderfully soothing and filling.

Serves 8

Combine the chicken stock and seasonings in a large pot and simmer.

Heat the oil in a frying pan and sauté the okra for 10 minutes. Add the onion, celery, green pepper, and garlic and cook for another 20 minutes.

Add the brown sugar, stewed tomatoes, and vegetable mixture to the broth and simmer for 1 hour, uncovered.

Season to taste with salt and pepper, Worcestershire, and Tabasco.

Add the shrimp, crab, chicken, or all three and heat.

Serve in bowls with hot cooked rice.

## Ingredients

2 quarts chicken stock
2 bay leaves
4 whole cloves
Pinch of cayenne pepper
3 tablespoons oil
1 pound fresh okra, sliced
3 cups chopped onion
1 cup chopped celery
1 green bell pepper, chopped
1 tablespoon minced garlic
2 tablespoons brown sugar
1 can (1 pound) stewed tomatoes, undrained
Salt and pepper to taste
1 tablespoon Worcestershire sauce
Tabasco to taste
1 pound cooked shrimp, crab, or diced chicken

## Hint

If fresh okra is unavailable, use a can of okra that has been well drained. Do not sauté the canned okra. Add the okra with the stewed tomatoes.

# CHICKEN GUMBO SOUP

## Ingredients

¼ cup salt pork, cut into
    ¼-inch pieces
2 tablespoons fat, drained
    from the pork
2 teaspoons grated onion
1 cup cooked chicken, cut
    into small pieces
¼ cup canned okra
3½ cups chicken broth
1 cup canned tomatoes,
    broken into 1-inch pieces
½ teaspoon salt
3 tablespoons cooked rice

*This* is a favorite from the deep south.

**Serves 4**

Sauté the salt pork until it is crisp and brown. Drain and save the fat. Reserve the cooked salt pork.

Return 2 tablespoons of fat to the frying pan and add the onion and chicken. Simmer for 5 minutes.

Add the okra, sautéed pork, chicken broth, and tomatoes. Heat to boiling. Add the salt and cooked rice and serve at once.

# VEGETABLE STEW

*T*his is thoroughly satisfying as well as healthy. You can use any combination of vegetables, or use a large can of tomato juice in place of the chicken broth.

**Serves 12**

Use a deep pot to fry the chopped onion in the olive oil until it is transparent.

Add all the vegetables and the chicken stock to the pot and bring to a boil. Season to taste. Cover the pot and turn off the heat. Let sit for 15 minutes. The vegetables should stay crisp. Serve hot.

Season with salsa if you want your soup spicy hot.

## Ingredients

1 large onion, diced

2 tablespoons olive oil

1 bunch leeks, carefully washed and sliced

1 large potato, peeled and diced

3 carrots, sliced

2 stalks celery or bok choy, sliced

2 cups finely shredded cabbage

2 tomatoes, peeled and chopped

1 green bell pepper, chopped

1 can (5 ounces) sliced water chestnuts

1 cup frozen peas

1 can (15½ ounces) corn, drained

4 cans (15 ounces each) chicken stock

Salt and pepper to taste

Salsa, optional

# ONION SOUP

## Ingredients

4 tablespoons (½ stick)
   butter
1 tablespoon olive oil
8 large onions, thinly sliced
¼ cup flour
4 cups chicken stock
4 cups beef stock
¼ cup dry white wine
2 tablespoons brandy
Salt and pepper to taste
8 slices French bread,
   toasted
1 pound Swiss cheese,
   thickly sliced

*T*his is soul-satisfying comfort food.

Serves 8

In a deep pot that has a lid, heat the butter and olive oil and brown the sliced onions slowly over low heat. Stir occasionally for 30 minutes. Cover the pot between stirrings.

Remove the pot lid and continue cooking for a few minutes until the onions are golden. Add the flour to the onions, stirring constantly. Add the chicken and beef stock and bring the soup to a boil. Just before serving, add the white wine and brandy. Season to taste with salt and pepper. If you use canned broth eliminate the salt.

Preheat the broiler. Fill individual soup bowls with the onion soup and float a slice of toasted French bread on top of the soup. Cover the bread with the sliced Swiss cheese and place the individual bowls under the broiler until the cheese is bubbly, has completely covered the top of the onion soup, and is crusty.

# CHICKEN SOUP WITH MATZO BALLS

*T*his is the Jewish cure for almost everything. I was delighted to discover that the Chinese have their own version of this cure-all called "Chook."

**Serves 8**

In a large soup pot, combine all the stock ingredients. Bring the mixture to a boil, reduce the heat, cover the pot, and simmer for 1 hour or until the chicken is tender.

Remove the chicken and vegetables with a slotted spoon. Refrigerate the soup until it is well chilled, at which time you can easily remove the congealed fat that has formed on top of the soup.

Beat the eggs well and stir in the salt and matzo meal. Add the melted fat and 4 tablespoons broth and mix well. Cover and chill for at least 2 hours.

In a large pot, boil 8 cups of water. Drop the dough by the tablespoonful into the boiling water and cover the pot. Reduce the heat and simmer for 30 minutes or until the matzo balls have doubled in size and are floating on top of the water.

Meanwhile, in another large pot, bring the chicken stock to a simmer.

Remove the matzo balls from the water and place them in the hot chicken broth. Continue to simmer for an additional 30 minutes. Serve hot.

## *Ingredients*

**Chicken stock**

2 pounds of chicken pieces (necks, thighs, backs, or wings)

3 stalks celery

2 medium carrots, cut in large pieces

1 teaspoon salt

1/2 teaspoon pepper

6 cups water

1 large onion, cut in quarters

2 bay leaves

1 parsnip, optional

**Matzo balls**

4 eggs

1/2 teaspoon salt

1 cup matzo meal

4 tablespoons melted chicken fat or oil

4 tablespoons broth or water

# MUSHROOM BARLEY SOUP

## Ingredients

½ pound mushrooms, sliced (2 cups)

1 large onion, finely chopped

2 cloves garlic, minced

1 cup quick-cooking barley

½ teaspoon salt

½ teaspoon pepper

2 bay leaves

2 pounds beef bones or stew meat

8 cups water

4 large carrots, chopped

3 stalks celery, chopped

1 cup frozen peas

*T*his is my idea of comfort food on a cold night. If you like marrow, try to find some marrow bones and add them to the soup. This soup is very thick and satisfying. Serve it with warm bread and a salad.

**Serves 8**

In a large soup pot, combine all the ingredients and bring the mixture to a boil. Reduce the heat to a simmer and heat for 2 hours or until the beef is tender. Remove bones and bay leaves before serving.

# CHEDDAR CHEESE SOUP

*T*his is my daughter Toni's favorite. It's thick and creamy and very comforting.

**Serves 4 to 6**

In a soup pot, melt butter and cook the vegetables and garlic over light heat until the vegetables are tender. Stir in the flour. Add the chicken broth and salt. Cook, stirring frequently, until the mixture is thick and bubbly. Stir in the milk and the cheese.

Heat until the cheese is melted. Serve hot.

## Ingredients

2 tablespoons butter

2 carrots, sliced thin

1 small onion, finely chopped

2 stalks celery, finely chopped

1 teaspoon minced garlic

1/4 cup flour

1 cup chicken broth

1/4 teaspoon salt

2 cups light cream or milk

2 cups (8 ounces) shredded sharp Cheddar cheese

# FLUFFY DUMPLINGS

¹/₂ cup water

4 tablespoons (¹/₂ stick)
   butter

¹/₂ cup flour

1 teaspoon baking powder

Pinch of salt

2 eggs

**S**erve these with stewed chicken or in a vegetable soup.

**Makes 12 dumplings**

Bring the water and butter to a boil in a saucepan. In a measuring cup, mix the flour, baking powder, and salt. Add to the saucepan all at once—as if you were making cream puffs. Stir the mixture well until a ball is formed that doesn't separate.

Remove the mixture from the heat and allow it to cool slightly. Add the eggs, one at a time, beating well after each addition, until the mixture is smooth.

Dip a tablespoon into the soup or hot water before forming each dumpling in order to keep the batter from sticking to the spoon. Drop the mixture into boiling soup or stew by the tablespoonful. Cover the pot and simmer the dumplings for 20 minutes.

# HOT AND SOUR SOUP

*I*f your idea of comfort is hot and spicy, try this soup. This recipe, from Devorah Mann, will require a lot of preparation, but it is worth the effort.

**Serves 6**

Cut the red pepper into small strips. Chop the onions finely. Slice the bean curd into 1/2-inch cubes.

In a large pot, combine the chicken broth, chili sauce, and soy sauce. Bring the soup to a boil and simmer for 5 minutes, uncovered.

Blend the cornstarch into the water. When the soup comes to a boil, stir this mixture into the soup until the soup thickens. Add the mushrooms, turkey, chopped pepper, and water chestnuts and simmer for 5 minutes, uncovered.

Add the wine, vinegar, and oil to the soup. In a small cup, mix the beaten egg with 1 tablespoon of water. Stirring constantly, add the egg mixture to the hot soup. Add the chopped onions, bean curd, and shrimp and cook for 5 minutes or until the shrimp turns pink.

## Ingredients

1 small red bell pepper

8 green onions

8 ounces firm bean curd

8 cups chicken broth

1 teaspoon Chinese chili sauce

1/4 cup soy sauce

3 tablespoons cornstarch

5 tablespoons water

6 mushrooms, sliced

8 ounces uncooked ground turkey

1 can (5 ounces) water chestnuts, sliced

1/2 cup dry white wine

2 teaspoons vinegar

1 teaspoon sesame oil

1 egg, beaten

8 ounces uncooked shrimp, cleaned and deveined

# CHILI

## Ingredients

2 tablespoons olive oil

1 large onion, finely
chopped

2 pounds ground sirloin

½ cup chili powder

2 cans (28 ounces each)
Italian plum tomatoes,
crushed, undrained

1 cup beef broth

2 tablespoons minced garlic

2 bay leaves

Salt

Pepper

2 tablespoons brown sugar

1 tablespoon wine vinegar

2 cans (1 pound each) pinto
beans, drained, optional

*T*his is fast and easy and perfect for dinner or a chilly evening. You can eliminate the beans or cook your own. This chili is also wonderful served over sausage or hot dogs. Of course, it is always a crowd pleaser.

**Serves 8 hearty eaters**

In a large pot, heat the olive oil and brown the onion. When the onion is transparent, add the ground beef and stir until well browned. Drain off the fat.

Add the chili powder, tomatoes, broth, garlic, and bay leaves. Add salt and pepper to taste. Bring the mixture to a boil. Reduce the heat and simmer for 30 minutes. Stir in the brown sugar and the vinegar and adjust the seasonings. Add the beans if desired and simmer for 15 minutes.

## Hint

I like to prepare my chili at least a day in advance so that it can be chilled and any fat that appears can be removed. Reheat the chili and serve.

# VEGETARIAN CHILI

*7his* is spicy and comforting especially if you are on a fat-free diet. You may have to eliminate the cheese or use it sparingly, but this chili will still be delicious.

**Serves 6 to 8**

Rinse the beans. Place them in a large pot and cover them with 4 cups water. Bring this to a boil and simmer for 2 minutes. Remove the beans from the heat. Cover them and let them stand for 1 hour. If you prefer, you can soak the beans in the water overnight in a covered pan. Drain the water and replace with an equivalent amount of fresh water.

Use a large pot and combine the beans and their liquid with the remaining ingredients. Bring to a boil, cover the pot, and allow the mixture to simmer for 2 hours.

Serve hot with grated cheese.

## Ingredients

1 cup dry pinto beans

1 can (16 ounces) corn, undrained

1 can (5 ounces) tomato sauce

1 large onion, finely chopped

1 can (4 ounces) green chile peppers, rinsed, seeded, and chopped

1 tablespoon chili powder

1 teaspoon salt

2 teaspoons minced garlic

2 bay leaves

1/4 cup red wine

Grated cheese

# CHASENS' CHILI

## Ingredients

½ pound dry pinto beans

2 cans (20 ounces each)
  Italian plum tomatoes,
  undrained

2 teaspoons olive oil

2 large onions, chopped

2 large green bell peppers,
  chopped

⅓ cup chopped parsley

4 cloves garlic, minced

1 pound lean ground pork

1½ pounds coarsely ground
  beef

2 tablespoons chili powder

2 tablespoons salt

1 teaspoon pepper

1½ teaspoons ground
  cumin

Grated sharp Cheddar
  cheese, optional

Chasens was a famous Hollywood restaurant that is now closed. Elizabeth Taylor loved this chili and she had it shipped to her all over the world.

**Serves 6**

Wash the pinto beans and soak them overnight or at least 8 hours. Drain the water and simmer the beans in fresh water until they are tender. Add the tomatoes to the beans and simmer for an additional 10 minutes.

In another pan, heat the oil and sauté the onions and green peppers until tender, stirring frequently. Add the parsley and garlic.

Sauté the ground meats until well browned. Skim off any fat in the pan. Combine the meat with the cooked beans and the onion mixture. Add the spices, cover, and simmer for 1 hour.

Uncover the pot and simmer for an additional 30 minutes. This can be chilled and prepared several days in advance, which will give you a chance to skim off any fat.

Heat and serve with garlic bread and a bowl of grated sharp Cheddar cheese.

# CARROT SOUP

*T*his is actually lowfat and healthy, but since it is very comforting, served hot or cold, I'm going to include it. Ladies love it because it is colorful and delicious for a luncheon.

**Serves 6**

## Ingredients

3 tablespoons butter

2 pounds carrots, chopped

1 small onion, chopped

1 bay leaf

1 potato, peeled and
    chopped

6 cups chicken or vegetable
    stock

Salt and white pepper

Chopped mint for garnish

Sour cream and chopped
    parsley for garnish

Melt the butter in a large saucepan and cook the carrots and onions over low heat for about 10 minutes, covered.

Add the bay leaf, potato, and chicken stock and simmer for 40 minutes, covered, stirring occasionally.

Discard the bay leaf. Use a food processor or a blender to purée the soup in small batches if necessary. Add seasonings.

Serve hot or cold garnished with mint, or sour cream and parsley.

# MINESTRONE WITH MEATBALLS

## Ingredients

1 can (28 ounces) Italian
   tomatoes, chopped,
   undrained

2 cups shredded cabbage

2 small zucchini, sliced

1 can (12 ounces) corn,
   undrained

1 can (15 ounces) garbanzo
   beans, drained

3 carrots, sliced

1/2 pound mushrooms,
   sliced (2 cups)

2 stalks celery, sliced

1 medium onion, chopped

1 cup broken vermicelli (or
   other pasta), uncooked

1/2 cup dry red wine

2 tablespoons snipped
   parsley

2 instant bouillon cubes

1 teaspoon oregano,
   crushed

1/4 teaspoon basil, crushed

2 teaspoons garlic powder

1 1/2 teaspoons salt

*(continues)*

*F*or most people, soup is almost at the top of the list of comfort foods. This hearty soup is filling and satisfying. Serve it with hot French garlic bread.

**Serves 8**

In a large soup pot, combine the undrained tomatoes, cabbage, zucchini, undrained corn, garbanzo beans, carrots, mushrooms, celery, onion, uncooked pasta, red wine, parsley, bouillon cubes, oregano, basil, and 1 teaspoon of the garlic powder.

Add water, 1 teaspoon salt, and 1 teaspoon pepper and bring to a boil. Cover, reduce heat, and simmer for 15 minutes.

In a separate bowl combine the ground beef, egg, milk, bread crumbs, Worcestershire sauce, ½ teaspoon salt, dash of pepper, and remaining teaspoon garlic powder. Mix well. Shape into tiny meatballs.

Place the meatballs on a plate, cover with wax paper, and microwave for 5 minutes on high. Turn the meatballs, re-cover, and microwave for an additional 3 minutes on high. If you do not have a microwave, pan-brown the meatballs.

Drain the fat from the meatballs and add them to the soup. Cover the pot and cook for an additional 20 minutes or until the vegetables are tender.

Serve hot and pass freshly grated Parmesan cheese to sprinkle on the top of the soup.

4 cups water
1 teaspoon plus a dash of pepper
1 pound lean ground beef
1 beaten egg
¼ cup milk
⅓ cup dry bread crumbs
1 teaspoon Worcestershire sauce
Grated Parmesan cheese

## Hint

I use scissors to snip parsley, basil, mint, and other fresh herbs. This method is easier than chopping.

# NEW ENGLAND CLAM CHOWDER

## Ingredients

1 medium onion, finely
chopped

2 stalks celery, finely
chopped

1 tablespoon oil

4 tablespoons (1/2 stick)
butter

2 tablespoons flour

3 1/2 cups milk or light
cream

3 cans (6 ounces each)
minced clams and their
juice

3 large potatoes, boiled and
cubed

6 slices bacon, fried and
crumbled

Salt and pepper

*Y*es, indeed! This is comfort food, especially on a damp winter night. Use canned clams and you'll find this is easy to prepare.

**Serves 4**

Sauté the onion and celery in the oil until transparent and set aside.

Melt the butter and stir in the flour until smooth. Add the milk or cream and clam juice. Cook, stirring constantly, until thickened.

Add the cooked celery and onion, potatoes, clams, and crumbled bacon and season with salt and pepper to taste.

# MANHATTAN CLAM CHOWDER

*N*ew England Clam Chowder is white—this is red. They are both equally delicious and easy to prepare using canned clams.

**Serves 6**

Cook the bacon until it is almost crisp. Add the celery and onion and cook over medium heat until the onions are transparent.

Add 3 cups of water and the juice from the clams. Add the tomatoes with their juice, potato, salt, and thyme.

Cover the pot and simmer for 45 minutes. Blend together the flour and water and stir this mixture into the chowder to thicken. Bring to a boil and add the clams. Serve hot.

## Ingredients

4 slices bacon, cut into small pieces

1 cup finely chopped celery

1 cup finely chopped onion

3 cups water

2 cans (6 ounces each) chopped clams and their juice

1 can (16 ounces) peeled tomatoes, chopped, undrained

1 large potato, cooked and diced

1 teaspoon salt

¼ teaspoon thyme, crushed

2 tablespoons flour

2 tablespoons water

# CIOPPINO

## Ingredients

3 tablespoons olive oil

1½ cups chopped onion

3 cloves garlic, crushed

1 cup chopped celery

1 cup chopped green bell
   pepper

1 can (28 ounces) Italian
   plum tomatoes,
   undrained

2 cans (6 ounces each)
   tomato paste

½ teaspoon Italian
   seasoning

1 teaspoon salt

½ teaspoon pepper

2 cups water

1 cup dry red wine

4 pounds of mixed seafood:
   clams, oysters, shrimp,
   mussels, white fish, scal-
   lops, cooked crab, or
   cooked lobster

Cioppino is an Italian, tomato-based fish stew—the kind you get at Fisherman's Wharf in San Francisco. You eat it with thick slabs of warm Italian sourdough bread. I drool just thinking about eating this!

**Makes 3½ quarts**

In a large kettle, heat the oil and sauté the onion, garlic, celery, and green pepper. Cook until the onions are transparent. Chop the tomatoes with their juice and add them to the onion mixture. Add tomato paste, seasoning, salt, pepper, water, and wine. Heat to boiling.

Shell and devein the shrimp. If you are using clams, oysters or mussels, boil them for a few minutes until their shells open. Rinse them in cold water.

Add all the fish and shellfish to the soup mixture after cutting any large pieces to bite size. Boil gently for 5 minutes, then cool to serving temperature.

## Hint

This is delicious made with shrimp and crab, or chunks of fish without the shellfish.

# TOMATO SOUP

This is definitely comfort food. You can add chopped, diced chiles to make it hotter if you like.

Serves 8

Place the butter, carrots, and onions in a large pot. Cover and steam the vegetables for 15 minutes.

Add the tomatoes and baking soda to the vegetables. Add the milk and cream.

Reheat before serving, but do not boil. Season with salt and pepper and add diced chiles for a spicier soup.

## Ingredients

3 tablespoons butter

5 large carrots, grated

2 small onions, sliced

1/3 cup long grain rice, cooked

2 cans (16 ounces each) puréed tomatoes

1/2 teaspoon baking soda

4 cups milk or light cream, hot

1/2 cup heavy cream, warm

Salt and pepper to taste

Diced chiles, optional

## Hint

Serve this soup with the dumplings on page 68 for a real treat.

# STEW

## Ingredients

2 tablespoons olive oil

1½ pounds cubed beef, pork, veal, or lamb

2 teaspoons minced garlic

2 bay leaves

1 teaspoon salt

1 teaspoon freshly ground pepper

1 teaspoon prepared mustard

½ teaspoon herb of choice, optional

1 can (10½ ounces) chicken or beef broth

1 large potato, cut into chunks

6 cups chopped vegetables

2 tablespoons cornstarch

¼ cup water

*G*ood, old-fashioned stew served with hot bread and a salad. What could bring more comfort on a chilly night?

The trick is to make sure that the meat is thoroughly browned. Take your time and brown it on all sides. You can add any vegetables you like and change the flavor by substituting wine or beer for part of the broth.

**Serves 4**

In a large frying pan, heat the olive oil and brown the meat. Cook the meat until it is brown on all sides.

Add the garlic, bay leaves, salt, pepper, and mustard. Add herbs if desired.

...mixture in a large Dutch oven
...en or beef broth. Bring to a
...at, cover the pot, and sim-
...s tender. Beef takes about
..., and veal should be tender

...and vegetables. Cover and
...itional minutes.

Stir the cornstarch and water together, add to the stew, and stir until thick.

## Hint

I place the meat cubes in a plastic bag with 1 cup of flour and shake the bag until the meat is well coated before browning. You will need additional olive oil if you are browning the flour-drenched meat, but you can eliminate adding the corn-starch and water to the stew for thickening.

# SALADS

$7$he recipes in this section prove that salads can be fun, fattening, and delicious. Caesar salad (page 91) was an overwhelming favorite comfort food, as were creamy potato salad (page 85) and tender chicken salad (page 94).

The potluck salad (page 98) is a great picnic idea, especially if you can tell the participants what to bring and surprise them with the combined efforts.

# POTATO SALAD

𝒞reamy, delicious, and the perfect accompaniment to a sandwich even if you use fat-free mayonnaise. The following recipe is enough for 4 and you can multiply it if you are preparing it for a crowd.

**Serves 4**

Cut the potato into small cubes and mix with the remaining ingredients. Chill for at least 1 hour before serving. Sprinkle the chopped green onion on top of salad.

## Ingredients

1 extra-large potato, boiled until just tender and peeled

4 hard boiled eggs, chopped

3 stalks celery, finely chopped

1 cup mayonnaise

1 teaspoon garlic powder

1 teaspoon salt

1/2 teaspoon pepper

1 teaspoon dry mustard or 2 teaspoons Dijon mustard

1 tablespoon dill pickle relish

Chopped green onion for garnish

# CREAMY COLESLAW

## Ingredients

1 medium head green
   cabbage
1 green or red bell pepper,
   chopped
1 carrot, shredded
½ teaspoon salt
½ teaspoon pepper
½ cup white wine vinegar
2 tablespoons sugar
½ cup water
1½ cups mayonnaise

*P*erfect for a picnic or with fried chicken—
crunchy and comforting.

**Serves 6**

Shred the cabbage and add the remaining ingredients except for the mayonnaise. Refrigerate the coleslaw for one hour and then drain the
liquid and stir in the mayonnaise. Chill until
time to serve.

# CRAB LOUIS

*T*his salad is easy to prepare, elegant, and oh, so satisfying for crabmeat lovers.

**Makes 1 cup dressing and 4 salads**

Mix all the dressing ingredients together until well blended.

To assemble the salad, place shredded lettuce on four salad plates. Top the lettuce with crabmeat. Garnish with sliced egg, tomato, and cucumber.

Serve with Louis dressing.

## Ingredients

**Louis dressing**

⅓ cup mayonnaise

½ cup bottled chili sauce

2 tablespoons French dressing

½ teaspoon minced onion

½ teaspoon Worcestershire sauce

Salt and pepper

**Salad**

1 small head lettuce, shredded

2 cups fresh crabmeat (about 1 pound)

4 hard boiled eggs, peeled and sliced

2 tomatoes, quartered

1 medium cucumber, sliced

# ANTIPASTO SALAD

## Ingredients

1 cucumber, thinly sliced

1 small sweet onion, thinly
sliced

2 jars (6 ounces each) artichoke hearts, drained

1/4 pound thinly sliced
salami

1 can (7 1/4 ounces) ripe
olives, drained

1 green bell pepper, sliced
thinly

1/2 pound Mozzarella
cheese, cut into small
cubes (2 cups)

2 tomatoes, chopped

1/2 cup Italian salad dressing, or oil and vinegar

*T*his is an easy version of that famous Italian appetizer. This version is made ahead and stored in the refrigerator. It's perfect for a picnic dinner.

**Makes 1 quart**

Layer all the ingredients except the dressing in a 4-cup glass casserole. Pour dressing over everything.

Cover and refrigerate for several hours. Serve on lettuce if desired.

# WALDORF SALAD

*R*emember this crisp, tart, and juicy salad? It's not as popular anymore, but it's still wonderful.

**Serves 6**

## Ingredients

2 tart apples, peeled, cored, and diced

1 cup finely chopped celery

½ cup chopped walnuts

¼ cup mayonnaise

1 tablespoon sugar

1 teaspoon lemon juice

Dash of salt

½ cup whipping cream, whipped, or 1 cup whipped topping

Combine the apples, celery, and nuts. Blend together the mayonnaise, sugar, lemon juice, and salt. Fold in the whipped cream and the apple mixture.

Chill and serve.

# AMBROSIA SALAD

## Ingredients

1 cup diced, peeled orange

2 bananas, peeled and
    sliced

1 cup seedless green grapes

1/4 cup chopped pitted
    dates

3 tablespoons lemon juice

1 cup mayonnaise

1 cup whipping cream,
    whipped

1/4 cup flaked coconut

*A*nother oldie but goodie!

**Serves 6**

Combine the fruits and sprinkle with lemon juice. Chill.

Fold the mayonnaise and whipped cream together and fold into the chilled fruit mixture. Top with coconut.

# CAESAR SALAD

*7his* is my favorite salad. Serve it plain or with grilled chicken or beef strips. Use the dressing as a marinade for grilling fish and meat. For a grandstand effect, prepare this right in front of your guests!

**Serves 4**

Place the mustard, lemon juice, garlic, egg yolks, anchovies, and Worcestershire sauce in a blender and process for 1 minute.

With the blender on its lowest speed, add the olive oil and mix until the dressing is well blended. Pour it into a jar, cover, and refrigerate for up to a week.

Wash and dry the romaine lettuce. Tear the lettuce into chunks.

Use a wooden salad bowl. Spread ½ cup of the dressing on the sides of the salad bowl and add the romaine leaves. Toss them to cover with the dressing from the side of the bowl.

Serve with Parmesan cheese, anchovy strips, croutons, and a spoonful of chopped egg.

## Ingredients

2 tablespoons Dijon
 mustard
Juice of 1 lemon
3 cloves garlic, peeled
2 large egg yolks
8 anchovies
1 teaspoon Worcestershire
 sauce
¾ cup olive oil
1 head romaine lettuce
2 tablespoons freshly grated
 Parmesan cheese
Anchovy strips for garnish
1 cup croutons for garnish
Chopped cooked egg for
 garnish

## Hint

Fresh garlic works best for this salad. If you hate anchovies, check out the next recipe, Almost Caesar Salad.

# ALMOST CAESAR SALAD

## Ingredients

1 head romaine lettuce,
   washed and broken into
   pieces
1 egg
1 teaspoon garlic powder
4 tablespoons sour cream
$1/2$ teaspoon ground
   pepper
3 tablespoons olive oil
1 teaspoon wine vinegar
1 cup seasoned croutons
1 cup freshly grated Parmesan cheese

*A* great Caesar salad for people who hate anchovies.

**Serves 6**

Place the lettuce in a large salad bowl.

Using a food processor or mixer, combine the egg, garlic powder, sour cream, pepper, oil, and vinegar for the dressing. Mix until well blended.

Just before serving, toss the dressing and lettuce together. Sprinkle with croutons and Parmesan cheese.

# PASTA SALAD

*B*y any name, this is a combination of vegetables and pasta, served cold. Add chopped meats,
onions, nuts, or whatever you like best.

**Serves 6**

Combine all the ingredients except the lettuce and gently toss until the pasta is completely
coated. Serve on a bed of lettuce.

## Ingredients

8 ounces shell-shaped
    pasta, cooked and
    drained, at room
    temperature
$1/2$ cup mayonnaise
$1/4$ cup sour cream
1 red bell pepper, finely
    chopped
1 green bell pepper, finely
    chopped
1 teaspoon salt
$1/2$ teaspoon garlic powder
1 teaspoon Worcestershire
    sauce
$1/2$ cup seedless green
    grapes
Lettuce, optional

# CHICKEN SALAD

## Ingredients

2 pounds chicken breasts, skinned

4 stalks celery, finely diced

1 teaspoon prepared mustard

1/2 teaspoon salt

1/4 teaspoon pepper

6 hard boiled eggs, diced

1/2 cup mayonnaise

2 tablespoons finely chopped parsley, optional

1/4 cup sour cream, optional

Salt and pepper to taste

The trick to cooking tender (not chewy) chicken is to let the chicken cool in the cooking broth before chopping it.

**Serves 4**

Cover the chicken pieces with water and bring to a boil. When the water is boiling, cover the pot and boil gently for 18 minutes. Then let the chicken cool in the broth for 2 hours. Remove the bones and cut or tear the chicken into chunks.

Mix all the ingredients together and season to taste with salt and pepper. Serve chilled.

## Hint

Add chopped nuts or Chinese crisp noodles as a topping for the salad.

.

# BROWN DERBY SALAD

*T*he Brown Derby in Hollywood is long gone. The building was shaped like a derby hat. However, there is a replica at Universal Studios in Orlando, Florida. If you like Cobb salad, you'll love this.

**Serves 6**

Place the shredded lettuce in a large salad bowl. On the lettuce arrange a row each of chicken, tomatoes, eggs, bacon, and cheese. Surround with slices of avocado.

Combine all the ingredients for the dressing in a blender and process until well mixed.

Toss the salad at the table with Brown Derby dressing.

## Ingredients

1 head Boston lettuce, shredded

2 chicken breasts, cooked, chilled, and diced

2 medium tomatoes, diced

4 hard boiled eggs, chopped

8 slices bacon, cooked crisp and crumbled

4 ounces Roquefort cheese, crumbled

2 medium avocados, halved and cut into thin wedges

**Brown Derby dressing**

1/2 cup red wine vinegar

1 tablespoon lemon juice

1 teaspoon pepper

1 teaspoon salt

1/2 teaspoon sugar

1/2 teaspoon dry mustard

1 1/2 teaspoons Worcestershire sauce

1 clove garlic, minced

1 cup salad oil

# SHRIMP SALAD

## Ingredients

1 pound small shrimp,
    cooked, shelled, and
    cooled
4 hard boiled eggs,
    chopped
1 cup chopped celery
¼ cup chopped green
    onion
Mayonnaise
1 tablespoon lemon juice
1 can (3 ounces) chow mein
    noodles
Avocado slices for garnish

*S*imilar to a shrimp cocktail but spread out on lettuce. This can serve as a luncheon entrée.

**Serves 4**

Combine the shrimp, eggs, celery, green onion, and just enough mayonnaise to bind the mixture together.

Add the lemon juice and carefully fold in the chow mein noodles. Garnish with avocado slices.

# LAYERED SALAD

7he perfect party salad because it looks wonderful and can be prepared a day ahead.

**Serves 8**

Use a large glass bowl—the kind you would use for a trifle dessert. This salad is visually beautiful.

Mix together the mayonnaise and sour cream in a small bowl and set aside. Layer the remaining ingredients except the cheese, and top each section with some of the mayonnaise mixture. Cover the entire top of the salad with the mayonnaise mixture and the grated cheese.

Cover with plastic wrap and refrigerate until time to serve. Toss the salad in front of your guests. Very impressive.

## Ingredients

1/2 cup mayonnaise

1/2 cup sour cream

1 head Boston lettuce, washed and broken into small pieces

1 cucumber, thinly sliced

1 package (10 ounces) frozen peas

1 pound bacon, fried crisp and crumbled

1 large red onion, sliced very thin and crisped in cold water

4 hard boiled eggs, chopped

3 large tomatoes, diced

12 fresh mushrooms, sliced

4 ounces Cheddar cheese, grated (1 cup)

# POTLUCK SALAD

## Ingredients

**Dressing**

1 cup olive oil

½ cup white wine vinegar

Reserved juice from the
   artichoke hearts

½ teaspoon dry mustard

1 teaspoon garlic powder

1 teaspoon sugar

Salt and pepper to taste

**Salad**

3 jars (6 ounces each) marinated artichoke hearts,
   chopped (reserve juice)

1 pound sliced mushrooms
   (4 cups)

3 pounds cooked chicken or
   turkey breast, diced

2 pounds cooked ham,
   diced

2 pounds sharp Cheddar
   cheese, grated

2 pounds bacon, fried and
   crumbled

12 hard boiled eggs,
   chopped

1 pound hard Italian salami,
   diced

3 ripe avocados, diced

*(continues)*

This is a group effort for a party or picnic. Everyone brings a part of the ingredients and someone brings a big wooden salad bowl. The ingredients are tossed together with the dressing. Serve with warm biscuits and sangría, and brownies for dessert.

**Serves 18 to 24**

Mix all the dressing ingredients together.

Marinate the artichokes and sliced mushrooms in the dressing for several hours or overnight.

At serving time, mix all the remaining ingredients in a huge wooden salad bowl and toss with the dressing, marinated artichoke hearts, and mushrooms.

1 can (7¾ ounces) black olives, pitted, drained, and sliced

2 bunches radishes, sliced thin

2 cucumbers, sliced thin

2 pints cherry tomatoes, halved

¼ pound pine nuts

6 heads of lettuce, preferably different kinds, torn into bite-size pieces

# SANDWICHES

*G*rilled cheese sandwiches were the hands-down winner on the comfort food questionnaire. I've included that recipe as well as others you mentioned.

Better stock up on napkins. Most of the following recipes will literally melt in your mouth as they run down your chin.

# SLOPPY JOES

*M*essy to eat but delicious. Wonderful served as Coney Island sandwiches (page 107).

**Serves 4**

Fry the ground beef and onion until the meat is browned and the onions are soft. Drain off any excess fat.

Add the tomato soup, water, mustard, salt, pepper, chili powder, paprika, hot sauce, and garlic powder. Simmer for 15 minutes, stirring occasionally. Serve on toasted buns.

## Ingredients

1 pound lean ground beef

1 small onion, chopped

1 can (10¾ ounces) condensed tomato soup

¼ cup water

1 tablespoon prepared mustard

½ teaspoon salt

¼ teaspoon pepper

½ teaspoon chili powder

½ teaspoon paprika

Dash of hot sauce

1 teaspoon garlic powder

4 hamburger buns, toasted

# THE ALL-AMERICAN HAMBURGER

## Ingredients

1½ pounds lean ground
    beef
1 teaspoon salt
¼ teaspoon pepper
1 teaspoon garlic powder or
    minced garlic
4 hamburger buns, split
    and toasted
4 slices tomato
4 slices sweet onion
Pickle relish or dill pickle
    slices
Mayonnaise or Thousand
    Island dressing
Mustard
Catsup

*A*mericans probably consume more hamburgers than any other food. There is nothing more delicious than a big juicy hamburger—unless it's a big cheeseburger. You can pan fry, broil, or grill your hamburgers.

**Serves 4**

Mix the ground beef with the salt, pepper, and garlic powder. Shape into 4 patties about 1 inch thick.

Pan-fry the meat over medium heat for about 8 minutes on each side for medium, 10 minutes for well done, or until the meat is done to your preference.

Place each burger on a toasted roll and top with your choice of tomato, onion, relish, mayonnaise, mustard, and catsup.

## Hint

The only way to improve on a hamburger is to add cheese: Monterey Jack, Cheddar, blue cheese, or Swiss. Place a slice of cheese on top of each hamburger while the meat is still hot and the cheese will melt

For another variation, when you shape the patties, fold a slice of cheese inside the meat and remember to seal the edges so that the cheese doesn't melt and leak out.

# PATTY MELT SANDWICH

## Ingredients

1 hamburger, cooked
    medium well
1 thick slice aged sharp
    Cheddar cheese
2 slices French bread,
    sliced about ½ inch thick
Butter for frying
Pickles
Mustard

*I*magine biting into a juicy hamburger covered with sharp, aged Cheddar cheese and pan-fried in butter on French bread. Imagine the calories!

**Serves 1**

Assemble the sandwich by placing the hamburger and cheese between two slices of bread.

Heat the butter in a frying pan (use clarified butter, page 228, to prevent smoking). Fry the sandwich on both sides in butter until the sandwich is golden brown on both sides.

Serve with pickles and mustard.

# CONEY ISLAND SANDWICHES

*M*y son Howard was mad about these when he was young—I still am.

**Serves 4**

## Ingredients

4 hot dog buns
1 pound all-beef hot dogs
2 cups Sloppy Joe mixture
  (page 103)
Chopped onion, optional
Mustard
Pickle relish
Grated cheese

Toast the hot dog buns while you are cooking the hot dogs. Microwave, barbecue, pan-fry, or boil the hot dogs until hot.

Place a hot dog in a roll and spoon on the Sloppy Joe sauce. Serve with condiments and chocolate milk shakes.

# REUBEN SANDWICH

## Ingredients

2 slices rye bread
Russian dressing
3 ounces thinly sliced
    corned beef
    (approximately)
Sauerkraut to taste, well
    drained
1 large slice Swiss cheese
Butter

*T*his is my buddy Bill's favorite sandwich. It requires lean, high-quality corned beef, but you can substitute turkey or ham for the corned beef.

**Serves 1**

Spread the slices of rye bread with Russian dressing and pile on some corned beef. You can use a thin layer of meat or pile it high. Pile the sauerkraut over the meat and top with a slice of Swiss cheese. Cover with another slice of rye bread that has been spread with Russian dressing.

Butter the outside of the top and bottom pieces of bread and place the whole sandwich in a heated skillet. When the bread is fried on one side, turn the sandwich over and fry the other side of the sandwich.

The filling should be hot and the cheese melted. Serve at once.

# MONTE CRISTO SANDWICH

*7*his is my son Daniel's idea of perfection. You can substitute sliced turkey or ham for the corned beef.

**Serves 1**

Combine the milk and egg and beat until well mixed.

Make a sandwich by placing the meat and cheese between the two slices of bread. Soak the sandwich, one side at a time, in the egg mixture.

Melt the butter in a frying pan over medium heat. When the bread has absorbed the egg mixture, place it in the pan and fry one side at a time until both sides are golden brown. Serve hot with homemade potato chips (page 206).

## Ingredients

1/4 cup milk

1 egg, well beaten

3 ounces thinly sliced corned beef

1 slice Jack or Swiss cheese

2 slices rye bread

2 tablespoons butter, clarified if possible

## Hint

If you want a more interesting sandwich, spread mustard on the bread slices before piling on the meat and cheese, or add pickle relish, sliced pickles, tomato slices, or a slice of onion.

# BACON, LETTUCE, AND TOMATO SANDWICH (BLT)

## Ingredients

8 slices toast

¼ cup mayonnaise

12 slices tomato

12 slices bacon, cooked crisp

4 lettuce leaves

*T*his is the original bacon sandwich. A customer in a bagel shop told me it is her primary comfort food. Bacon on a bagel?

**Serves 4**

For each sandwich, spread mayonnaise on 1 piece of toast. Cover with 3 slices of tomato and 3 slices of bacon. Top with 1 lettuce leaf. Top with second slice of toast. Cut in half and serve.

# CLUB SANDWICH

*A*nother old favorite still seen on menus because it gives lots of people pleasure.

**Serves 4**

For each sandwich, spread mayonnaise on 2 slices of bread. Place sliced turkey on the first slice of bread and top with another slice of bread spread with mayonnaise.

Add 3 slices of bacon, 3 slices of tomato, and top with a leaf of lettuce. Place another slice of bread on top.

Cut in half and serve with homemade potato chips (page 206), or deep-fried vegetable chips (page 216).

## Ingredients

12 slices white bread

¼ cup mayonnaise

½ pound sliced turkey breast

12 slices bacon, cooked crisp

4 lettuce leaves

12 slices tomato

# GRILLED CHEESE SANDWICH

## Ingredients

2 slices bread, your choice
1 thick slice Cheddar
   cheese
Butter

## Hint

You can add sliced tomatoes, onion, or chopped chiles— or really go for it with 3 slices of crisp bacon.

*A* very popular comfort food choice. Choose aged or mild Cheddar or your favorite cheese and then go for it.

**Serves 1**

Butter both sides of each slice of bread. Melt 1 tablespoon of butter in a hot frying pan (clarified butter won't smoke, but if you are in a hurry it won't matter).

Place the cheese between the bread slices and place the sandwich in the hot frying pan. Reduce the heat to medium and cook until the sandwich is toasty brown on both sides and the cheese has melted.

# GRILLED PEANUT BUTTER AND BANANA SANDWICH

*T*his is probably the ultimate fattening sandwich—but this book is about taste and comfort, not calories.

**Serves 1**

Butter bread, heavier on one side than the other. Spread peanut butter on one slice of bread and place slices of banana over the peanut butter.

Press the slices of bread together and fry the sandwich, turning it so that it is toasty brown on both sides.

## Ingredients

2 slices white or egg bread
Butter
Peanut butter, crunchy or
   smooth
1 banana, sliced

## Hint

You can add raisins or crisp bacon or both. This sandwich is great with milk.

# FRENCH DIP SANDWICHES

## Ingredients

1 package au jus mix, *or*
  2 cups roast beef gravy
2 pounds sliced roast beef
8 crusty French rolls, sliced
  lengthwise
Butter
Mustard
Mayonnaise
Horseradish

*T*he perfect solution to leftover roast beef. Slice it as thin as possible and allow at least 3 ounces of beef per sandwich.

**Serves 8**

Prepare the au jus mix according to the package directions or prepare 2 cups of roast beef gravy.

Place the meat on buttered French rolls and place them in a microwave dish. Cover the sandwiches lightly with plastic wrap and microwave them on high for 15 seconds per roll.

Pour the gravy into individual bowls and give one to each person so that they can dip their sandwich into the gravy.

Pass the mustard, mayonnaise, and horseradish.

# MAIN DISHES

$7$he dishes I consider to be entrées include everything you told me you loved, from breakfast through dinner. As my son Daniel said, I only serve entrées and desserts—several of each at every meal.

Most of these recipes are high calorie, high fat, high cholesterol, and very delicious. I would rather have a spoonful of something decadently delicious than a platter full of something healthful and bland. Wouldn't you?

# SOUR CREAM ENCHILADAS

*7*alk about creamy and delicious! This is from Kathy Sikora's private collection. Use mild chiles if your taste buds don't appreciate the hot ones.

**Serves 6**

Preheat the oven to 350°F. Butter a 9 × 12-inch baking dish.

Following the directions on page 94 for making chicken salad, cook the chicken in water until tender. Remove the skin and cut the chicken into bite-size pieces. Save the broth for another recipe.

In a large pot, mix together the soup, sour cream, onion, garlic, and chiles and simmer for 5 minutes.

In another skillet, heat the oil. Cook each tortilla in the oil until soft, about 1 to 2 minutes. Drain on paper towels.

Top each softened tortilla with chicken pieces and 2 tablespoons of the soup mixture. Roll up the tortillas.

Arrange the rolled and filled tortillas in the prepared baking dish and pour the remaining soup mixture over the enchiladas.

Top with the shredded cheese and bake, covered, for 20 minutes. Uncover and bake an additional 10 minutes. Serve hot.

## Ingredients

1 1/2 pounds chicken breasts
2 cans (10 1/2 ounces each) cream of chicken soup
1 cup sour cream
1 1/2 teaspoons minced onion
1 teaspoon minced garlic
2 cans (4 ounces each) chopped green chiles
1/2 cup vegetable oil
12 tortillas
1/2 pound sharp Cheddar cheese, grated (2 cups)

## Hint

Instead of softening the tortillas in oil, wrap each tortilla in a moistened paper towel and heat in the microwave for 20 seconds on high to soften.

# BEEF TACOS

## Ingredients

1 pound lean ground beef

2 tablespoons chopped
mild red chile pepper

1 clove garlic, finely minced

½ teaspoon salt

½ teaspoon cumin

¼ teaspoon oregano

1 Spanish onion, diced

1 medium tomato, diced

2 cups shredded lettuce

2 cups grated cheese (½
Jack and ½ Cheddar)

Salsa

## Hint

You can replace the beef with shredded roast pork or beef, chicken, hard boiled eggs, cooked chorizo sausage, shrimp, flaked fish, guacamole, vegetables, or frijoles (refried beans), which are also available, heaven forbid, in a tasty, fat-free, canned version.

*M*ake it easy on yourself—buy the prepared taco shells or use the tostado crisps.

**Makes 12 tacos**

Crumble the beef into a frying pan and brown. Drain off the fat and add the pepper, garlic, salt, cumin, and oregano and stir until well blended.

Preheat the oven to 450°F. Fill the taco shells with 3 tablespoons of the meat mixture, onion, and cheese. Place the filled tacos on an ungreased cookie sheet and heat in the hot oven for 10 minutes or until the shells are crisp and the cheese is melted.

Add shredded lettuce and tomato and pass the salsa.

# QUESADILLAS

*T*his is the Mexican version of a grilled cheese sandwich. It can be made using a broiler but these are most delicious fried in butter. You can also serve these as a main course with refried beans and Spanish rice, or cut them into triangles and serve them as appetizers.

**Makes 4 quesadillas**

Preheat the broiler.

Place the tortillas on a cookie sheet and brush the tops with melted butter. Turn the tortillas over and divide the cheese evenly on top of the tortillas. Top the cheese with another tortilla. Brush the top of the second tortilla with melted butter.

Place the quesadillas under the broiler until golden brown. Turn and broil the bottom tortilla. Serve hot with guacamole, sour cream, salsa, and chopped chiles.

If you fry the quesadillas in butter, place the grated cheese on half of the tortilla, fold it in half and fry both sides in butter until the tortilla is browned on both sides and the cheese is melted.

## Ingredients

8 (8-inch) flour tortillas
3 tablespoons melted butter
1 pound Monterey Jack cheese, grated (4 cups)
Guacamole
Sour cream
Salsa
Chopped chiles

# CHILES RELLENOS

## Ingredients

1 pound Cheddar cheese,
  grated (4 cups)
1 pound Monterey Jack
  cheese, grated (4 cups)
1 can (7 ounces) green
  chiles, sliced open with
  the seeds removed
½ cup milk
4 eggs
2 tablespoons flour
Salt and pepper to taste

*M*y buddy Bill thinks of this as his comfort food. If you are dieting, don't think of it at all. This is a spicy combination of melted cheeses and chiles. Wonderful!

**Serves 8**

Preheat the oven to 350°F. Butter a 9 × 13-inch baking pan and layer with the cheeses and chiles. Combine the milk, eggs, and flour and drizzle this over the cheese-chili mixture.

Bake for 45 minutes until golden brown and puffy. Cut into squares and serve hot.

# HUEVOS RANCHEROS

*I* think of most Mexican food as comfort food. I like it hot and spicy. You can make your own variation of this and serve it for breakfast, brunch, or whenever you are in the mood.

**Serves 6**

In a large skillet, heat the oil and fry the tortillas on both sides for 1 to 2 minutes until soft. Drain and place each tortilla on a plate. Heat the refried beans in a microwave for 5 minutes, and place a heaping tablespoon of the beans on the hot tortillas.

Place a fried egg on top of the beans, cover the egg with the grated cheese, and top with coriander, tomato, and onion. Pass a bowl of salsa to pour over the huevos rancheros.

## Ingredients

3 tablespoons oil

6 tortillas

1 can (16 ounces) refried beans

6 fried eggs, sunny-side up

4 ounces Cheddar cheese, grated (1 cup)

1 teaspoon chopped coriander, optional

1 large tomato, chopped

1 small onion, chopped

2 cups prepared salsa

# TAMALE PIE

*Ingredients*

1¹/₂ cups cold water

1¹/₂ cups yellow cornmeal

¹/₂ teaspoon salt

2 cups boiling water

1 pound ground chuck

¹/₂ cup chopped onion

2 tablespoons flour

1 teaspoon chili powder, or
    more for a spicier dish

1 can (1 pound) tomatoes,
    chopped, undrained

1 can (8 ounces) tomato
    sauce

1 can (8¹/₄ ounces) corn,
    drained

¹/₂ pound Cheddar cheese,
    grated (2 cups), optional

*A*lmost everyone loves this inexpensive dinner that is really quite simple to prepare.

**Serves 6**

Preheat the oven to 350°F.

Mix the cold water and cornmeal together. Add the salt and the cornmeal mixture to the boiling water. Stirring constantly, bring to a boil. Cover the pan and simmer for 10 minutes, stirring often.

Cover the sides and bottom of a well-buttered 8-cup baking dish with the cooked cornmeal mush.

Fry the beef and onion together until the beef is crumbly and brown. Add the flour, chili powder, tomatoes, tomato sauce, and corn. Pour this mixture into the baking dish lined with the cornmeal mush. Bake for 45 minutes.

Sprinkle grated cheese on top of the tamale pie before serving.

# BURRITOS

*Ingredients*

$\mathcal{T}$his recipe is from Nan Wineinger, who makes burritos often. She uses the largest flour tortillas available and then freezes them.

**Makes 12 big burritos**

2 pounds lean ground beef

1 onion, finely chopped

3 cloves garlic, minced

1/2 pound mushrooms, sliced (2 cups)

1 large green bell pepper, chopped

2 medium carrots, grated

4 medium zucchini, sliced thin

2 large potatoes, grated

12 large tortillas (10 to 12 inches across)

1/2 pound Cheddar cheese, grated (2 cups)

1/2 pound Monterey Jack cheese, grated (2 cups)

In a large skillet, cook the beef, onion, and garlic until the meat is brown. Drain off the excess fat. Stir in the remaining vegetables and simmer, uncovered, until the potatoes are cooked and the mixture is thick, about 30 minutes.

Cool the mixture. Place 1 cup of the meat mixture in the center of a tortilla and fold the tortilla so that the filling is completely enclosed.

Preheat the oven to 350°F and butter a 9 × 13-inch baking dish. Place the burritos on the baking dish and sprinkle with grated cheese. Bake for 15 to 20 minutes or until the cheese bubbles, and serve the burritos hot. Pass the salsa.

# CHILAQUILE WITH CHICKEN

## Ingredients

2 pounds chicken breast,
   boned and skinned

1 carrot, sliced

1 stalk celery, chopped

2 bay leaves

1/2 teaspoon salt

1/4 teaspoon pepper

2 medium onions,
   1 chopped and 1 cut
   in chunks

1 pound tomatillos (Mexi-
   can green tomatoes)

2 cloves garlic, minced

1/4 cup firmly packed fresh
   coriander

3 tablespoons lard plus additional for frying

1 cup chicken broth

12 corn tortillas, cut into
   strips

1/2 pound Monterey
   Jack cheese, grated
   (2 cups)

Avocado slices

*T*his casserole will serve a crowd, all shouting "olé."

**Serves 6**

Place the chicken, carrot, celery, bay leaves, salt, pepper, and 1 chopped onion in a pot and cover with water. Bring to a boil. Cover and boil for 18 minutes. Remove from heat and let the chicken cool in the pot for 2 hours.

Remove the chicken from the broth and cut into chunks. Set aside.

In a food processor or blender, combine the peeled tomatillos, 1 chunked onion, the garlic, and coriander and purée.

Melt 3 tablespoons of lard in a heavy skillet and add the purée. Cook and stir for about 5 minutes and slowly add in the chicken broth. Heat and adjust seasonings with salt and pepper.

Fry the tortilla pieces quickly in lard until they are crisp but not brown. Drain on paper towels.

Butter an 8 × 12-inch baking dish and layer the tortillas, chicken, and cheese and repeat until the ingredients are all used. Sprinkle a little more grated cheese on top of the casserole.

Cover and refrigerate at least 8 hours or overnight .

Preheat the oven to 350°F. Remove the casserole from the refrigerator, uncover, and bake 15 to 20 minutes or until bubbly.

Garnish with avocado slices.

## Hint

You can replace the lard with vegetable oil. I've also used packaged tortilla chips in this recipe and the result was wonderful.

# QUICHE

## Ingredients

1 prepared 9-inch pie crust
6 whole eggs
6 egg yolks
1 tablespoon Dijon mustard
1 tablespoon dry mustard
1 tablespoon white pepper
12 ounces Swiss cheese,
  grated (3 cups)
6 cups heavy cream,
  scalded

*T*his quiche is rich enough to serve as a complete luncheon or dinner if you serve it with a salad or fruit. It is my favorite quiche recipe. I use prepared pie crust that is already rolled out, but you can make your own.

**Serves 12**

Preheat the oven to 350°F.

Cut a 9-inch round of parchment paper and place in the bottom of a 9-inch springform pan. Line the bottom of the pan with the bottom of the crust. Reserve the rest of the crust. Bake for 10 minutes. Remove the pan from the oven and cool the crust. Press the remaining dough around the sides of the pan and attach it to the bottom crust.

While the crust is cooling, mix the remaining ingredients together. Pour them into the cooled crust. Bake the quiche at 350°F for 45 minutes or until it is set.

You can serve this quiche hot or cold.

# CHEESE PUDDING

*T*his is a sensational brunch or lunch dish. You can prepare it a day ahead. Add seafood or any meat to make the pudding even more satisfying.

**Serves 6**

Butter an 8-cup casserole or baking dish. Cut the bread into 1-inch cubes. Divide the bread and cheese into 3 parts.

Layer the baking dish with 1/3 of the bread and 1/3 of the cheese and repeat until all the bread and cheese are in the pan. Beat the eggs and milk together and add the seasonings.

Slowly pour this mixture over the bread and cheese and pour the melted butter on top. Cover the casserole and refrigerate overnight.

Preheat the oven to 350°F. Remove the casserole from the refrigerator while the oven is heating. Place the casserole in a larger pan. Pour 2 inches of water into the larger pan and bake, uncovered, for 1 hour and 15 minutes. The pudding will be brown on the top and puff up. Serve hot.

*Ingredients*

16 slices day-old white bread

1 pound sharp Cheddar cheese, grated (4 cups)

6 eggs

3 cups milk

1 teaspoon salt

1 teaspoon dry mustard

1/4 teaspoon paprika

1/2 teaspoon Worcestershire sauce

1/2 cup (1 stick) butter, melted

# CHEDDAR-BEER CHEESECAKE

## Ingredients

1 prepared 9-inch pie crust

2 pounds cream cheese at
    room temperature

1/2 pound extra-sharp
    Cheddar cheese, grated
    (2 cups)

1/2 cup sugar

4 eggs

2 egg yolks

1/4 cup beer or ale

1/4 cup heavy cream

*T*his is wonderful served as the main course for a luncheon. It is even more exciting served as a dessert because it is so unusual and a level above the traditional cheese board. I use prepared pie crust that is already rolled out, but you can make your own.

**Serves 12 to 18**

Preheat the oven to 350°F.

Cut a 9-inch round of parchment paper and place in the bottom of a 9-inch springform pan. Line the bottom of the pan with the bottom of the crust. Reserve the rest of the crust. Bake for 10 minutes. Remove the pan from the oven and cool the crust. Press the remaining dough around the sides of the pan and attach it to the bottom crust.

Preheat the oven to 500°F.

Beat the cheeses together until they are light and fluffy. Scrape the sides and bottom of the mixing bowl so that no chunks remain. Add the sugar and the eggs, one at a time. Add the egg yolks. Stir in the beer and the heavy cream.

Pour the filling into the prepared crust and bake the cheesecake for 10 minutes. Reduce the oven temperature to 250°F and bake the cheesecake for 1 hour or until a toothpick inserted in the center of the cheesecake comes out fairly clean. Serve warm or chilled.

## Ingredients

### Crust

½ cup fine dry bread
    crumbs
¼ cup grated Gruyère or
    Swiss cheese
¼ teaspoon dried dill weed

### Filling

3 tablespoons butter
1 medium onion, finely
    chopped
3 ½ packages cream cheese
    (8 ounces each), at room
    temperature
4 large eggs
½ cup grated Gruyère or
    Swiss cheese
⅓ cup half-and-half or
    whipping cream
Pinch of salt
1 tablespoon minced garlic
½ pound smoked salmon,
    coarsely chopped

# SMOKED SALMON CHEESECAKE

This is an outrageous cheesecake that can be served as an entrée or as a dessert. You can use the inexpensive end pieces of salmon for this delicacy.

**Serves 12 as an entrée or 18 as a dessert**

Preheat the oven to 325°F. Butter a 10-inch springform pan. Mix the crust ingredients together and sprinkle them over the bottom and the sides of the pan.

Melt the butter in a frying pan and add the onion. Sauté for 10 minutes or until the onion is transparent. Stir occasionally.

Use a mixer to beat the cream cheese until smooth. Add the eggs and ½ cup Gruyère cheese, the half-and-half, and the salt. Mix until very smooth. Blend in the garlic, salmon, and onions.

Pour the mixture into the prepared pan.

Cover the sides and the bottom of the pan with foil and set the cheesecake into a larger pan. Place both pans into the preheated oven and pour 2 inches of boiling water into the larger pan. Bake for 1 hour and 20 minutes. Turn off the heat and cool the cheesecake for about an hour with the oven door slightly open. Serve hot or at room temperature.

# CHEESE SOUFFLÉ

*T*his is a comfort on a cold day for lunch or dinner. You can use any cheese that you have on hand. If you plan ahead, buy Swiss cheese, Camembert, or Brie.

**Serves 3**

Preheat the oven to 350°F. Butter a 4-cup baking dish and dust it with Parmesan cheese.

In a medium saucepan, melt the butter and stir in the flour. Simmer for 2 or 3 minutes. Slowly add the milk and stir until the sauce is smooth and thick.

Add the egg yolks, one at a time. Add the cheese and stir until melted. Season with salt, pepper, hot sauce, and dry mustard and cool.

Whip the egg whites until they form soft peaks and fold the whites together with the cheese mixture. Pour the mixture into the prepared pan and bake for 30 minutes or until puffy and golden.

## Ingredients

Grated Parmesan cheese

2 tablespoons butter

2 tablespoons flour

1/2 cup milk

5 eggs, separated

4 ounces cheese, grated (1 cup)

Salt and pepper to taste

Hot sauce

Dry mustard

# RAREBIT

## Ingredients

1 pound sharp Cheddar
   cheese, grated (4 cups)
1 egg, slightly beaten
1/4 cup dry bread crumbs
4 toasted English muffins
   or 4 slices of toast

*R*arebit is great on English muffins and can be a brunch or supper served with a great salad. You can add sautéed onions and peppers or serve it plain.

**Serves 4**

Melt the Cheddar cheese in the microwave and stir it until it is smooth. Add the egg and bread crumbs and serve in a chafing dish or a fondue pot. Spoon over toast or English muffins.

# THE PERFECT OMELET

*The* trick to a perfect omelet is to cook the eggs in a frying pan until they are set. Place the toppings on the egg pancake and place the pan under the broiler. The omelet will puff up. Any variety of toppings can be used such as grated cheese, fresh herbs, caviar and sour cream, smoked salmon, crab or shrimp, salsa, mushrooms, tomatoes, and cooked sausage or bacon.

**Serves 1**

## Ingredients

2 eggs
¼ teaspoon salt
Pinch of freshly ground
  pepper
1 tablespoon milk or cream
1 tablespoon butter
Filling of choice

Preheat the broiler.

Beat the eggs, the seasonings, and the milk together until they are well mixed. Heat a frying pan over high heat. When the pan is hot, melt the butter and swirl it around so that the bottom of the pan is covered.

Pour in the egg mixture and lower the heat to medium. When the eggs are set, place the filling on top of the omelet and place the frying pan 4 inches under a hot broiler. Broil until the eggs have doubled in size and are puffed up and the toppings are toasty brown, about 5 to 10 minutes.

Fold the omelet in half and serve.

# EGG FOO YUNG

## *Ingredients*

### Pancakes

1 cup cooked shrimp, beef,
    chicken, or pork
1 can (1 pound) mixed Chi-
    nese vegetables, drained
6 eggs, well beaten
1 teaspoon salt
Oil for frying

### Gravy

2 cups water
1/4 cup soy sauce
2 tablespoons cornstarch
    dissolved in 1/4 cup water
1 teaspoon sugar

*T*his is a Chinese egg pancake that seems to have disappeared from the menu of Chinese restaurants. It is still my friend Bernie Fisher's idea of comfort food. Super easy to prepare and so delicious.

**Serves 4**

Combine all the pancake ingredients except the oil. Heat a small amount of oil in a frying pan and spoon in 1/4 cup of the mixture at a time.

When the pancakes are browned on the bottom, turn them gently and brown both sides.

While the pancakes are cooking, make the gravy. Blend the water and soy sauce. Add the cornstarch mixture and heat until slightly thickened. Serve over egg foo yung.

# FRITTATA

*A* frittata is a lovely, comfortable dish to serve. It can be served as an hors d'oeuvre or as a main dish. It's impressive and simple to prepare.

**Serves 9 as an entrée, more as hors d'oeuvres**

Preheat the oven to 350°F. Butter a 9 × 13-inch baking pan. You can use an 8-cup baking dish if you prefer.

Mix together the flour, baking powder, eggs, and butter and blend well. Add the cottage cheese, Jack cheese, and chopped chiles. Season to taste.

Pour the mixture into the prepared pan and bake for 45 minutes or until it is set. Cut into squares and serve.

## *Ingredients*

½ cup flour

1 teaspoon baking powder

6 eggs, slightly beaten

½ cup (1 stick) butter, melted and cooled

1 container (16 ounces) small curd cottage cheese

1 pound Monterey Jack cheese, grated (4 cups)

1 can (4 ounces) diced green chiles

Salt and pepper to taste

# FRIED CHICKEN WITH PAN GRAVY

## Ingredients

2 cups buttermilk

1 tablespoon hot sauce

2 chickens (4 pounds each), cut into serving-size pieces

2¼ cups flour

2 teaspoons salt

1 teaspoon pepper

Canola oil

4 cups milk

*A*lmost everyone loves fried chicken, especially with mashed potatoes and gravy. It's not fat-free or health food, but it is delicious!

**Serves 6**

Whisk together the buttermilk and hot sauce. Pour the buttermilk mixture over the chicken pieces in a large baking pan. Cover, refrigerate, and allow the chicken to marinate for at least 2 hours. You can leave the chicken in the refrigerator overnight if you prefer.

Mix together 2 cups of the flour, 1 teaspoon of the salt, and the pepper. Put the flour mixture in a large flat plate or a pie pan. Remove the chicken from the buttermilk, one piece at a time, and dredge the chicken in the flour mixture. Allow the coated chicken to rest on a rack for half an hour.

Heat the canola oil in a deep frying pan. The oil should come halfway up the chicken. Use a deep fryer if you have one.

When the oil is very hot (about 375°F), place the chicken into the oil and fry until the chicken is golden brown. Turn the chicken pieces and continue to fry until the chicken is golden brown on both sides.

Place the fried chicken on paper towels to drain. Skim the fat from the pan, reserving ¼ cup. Scrape the cracklings and any crisp pieces that remain from the bottom of the pan. Whisk the remaining ¼ cup of flour into the fat and scrapings.

Very slowly add the milk and the remaining 1 teaspoon of salt and, stirring constantly, allow the gravy to come to a simmer.

Simmer for about 10 minutes or until the gravy is thickened. Serve the gravy over the fried chicken and lumpy mashed potatoes (page 204).

# CASHEW CHICKEN

## Ingredients

1½ cups water

4 tablespoons dry sherry

2½ tablespoons cornstarch

2 tablespoons soy sauce

1 teaspoon instant chicken
   bouillon

4 whole chicken breasts

1 egg white

½ teaspoon salt

1 large carrot

6 green onions

3 stalks bok choy or celery

½ cup cashews

8 fresh mushrooms, sliced

½ can (4 ounces) sliced
   bamboo shoots, drained

*T*he only difficult thing about making Chinese food is the preparation of the ingredients. To make this far simpler, gather all the ingredients together well in advance.

Serves 4

Combine the water, 2 tablespoons of the sherry, 1½ tablespoons of the cornstarch, the soy sauce, and the chicken bouillon in a saucepan and heat until the mixture comes to a boil and becomes thick, about 5 minutes.

Remove the skin and the bones from the chicken and cut the chicken into 1-inch pieces. Combine the remaining 2 tablespoons of the sherry, 1 tablespoon of the cornstarch, the egg white, salt, and chicken pieces.

Pare the carrot and slice it thinly. Chop the green onions into 1-inch pieces. Cut the bok choy into diagonals about ½ inch thick.

Use a wok or a deep frying pan and heat the oil until it is very hot, about 375°F. Add half of the chicken pieces, one at time, and cook until light brown, about 5 minutes. Drain the chicken pieces on paper towels.

Stir-fry the cashews in the remaining oil for about 2 minutes. Drain the nuts on paper towels.

Add the carrot to the wok and stir-fry for 2 minutes. Add the remaining vegetables and stir-fry until they are crisp-tender, about 3 minutes. Mix in the chicken, nuts, and sauce and stir-fry until hot.

# CHICKEN CURRY

## Ingredients

1 small onion, chopped

½ green bell pepper, chopped

1 large potato, cooked and cubed

4 tablespoons (½ stick) butter

¼ cup slivered almonds

1 tablespoon curry powder

½ teaspoon salt

¼ teaspoon pepper

¼ cup flour

1 cup chicken broth

1 can (8 ounces) tomato sauce

1 teaspoon Worcestershire sauce

1 cup sour cream, at room temperature

4 cups cooked chicken or turkey cut into chunks

Hot cooked rice

Chopped raisins, nuts, or coconut, optional

*T*his is a special way of using up leftover chicken or turkey. It is my buddy Bill's idea of special comfort food.

Serves 4

Sauté the onions, green peppers, and potatoes in butter until the onions and peppers are soft. Add the slivered almonds. Add the curry powder, salt, and pepper and cook for 1 minute.

Stir in the flour and cook for 1 more minute. Add the broth and stir until smooth and thick.

Stir in the tomato sauce and Worcestershire sauce.

Combine the sour cream and chicken in a separate bowl and gradually add the sauce, stirring constantly. Return to pan and heat to serving temperature. Serve hot over rice with chopped nuts, raisins, coconut, or chutney as condiments.

# CHICKEN PARMIGIANA

*L*ots of people mention Italian food as their choice of comfort food. This recipe makes a dreamy, creamy entrée.

**Serves 6**

Preheat the oven to 325°F.

Mix together the eggs, salt, and pepper. Mix the bread crumbs with $1/2$ cup of the Parmesan cheese.

Dip the chicken into the eggs and then into the bread crumb mixture. If necessary, repeat this until the chicken is well coated. Place the coated chicken on wax paper.

Heat the oil in a skillet and brown the chicken breasts on both sides. Place the browned chicken into a large, flat baking dish.

If there is any grease left in the pan pour it off. Sauté the garlic for one minute. Add the tomato sauce, salt, and pepper. Add the bay leaf and soy sauce. Bring the mixture to a boil and then simmer for 10 minutes, stirring occasionally. Pour the sauce over the chicken. Sprinkle the remaining Parmesan cheese on top of the chicken. Cover the dish and bake for 30 minutes.

Just before serving, uncover the dish, remove the bay leaf, and place the sliced mozzarella cheese on top of the chicken. Place the dish under the broiler and heat until the cheese is melted.

## Ingredients

8 split chicken breasts, skinned, boned, and pounded thin

### Coating

2 eggs, slightly beaten
$1/2$ teaspoon salt
$1/8$ teaspoon pepper
1 cup dry, plain bread crumbs
$1 1/4$ cups grated Parmesan cheese

$1/2$ cup vegetable oil

### Sauce

2 cloves of garlic, minced
2 cups of tomato sauce
1 teaspoon salt
$1/2$ teaspoon pepper
1 bay leaf
1 tablespoon soy sauce

12 ounces mozzarella cheese, sliced

# CHICKEN POT PIE

## Ingredients

**Puff pastry dome**

1 package (10 ounces)
   frozen puff pastry or
   pastry shells, thawed
Garlic or salt, optional
1 egg yolk, slightly beaten

**Filling**

3 pounds chicken pieces
3 cups chicken broth
½ cup chopped onion
1 cup diced celery
6 tablespoons (¾ stick)
   butter, softened
6 tablespoons flour
1 cup heavy cream
1 teaspoon freshly ground
   pepper
1 package (10 ounces)
   frozen carrots and peas

*7his* recipe came from a collection by Kathleen Perry, *The Everyday Gourmet.* It is the very richest and best chicken pot pie ever and my grandchildren's all-time favorite food. Ms. Perry herself admits this is comfort food at its finest when dressed up with a puff pastry crust.

**Serves 4 generously**

Roll the pastry so that it is 2 inches wider than the 8-cup baking dish or the four 2-cup ovenproof serving bowls you are using for chicken pot pie. Sprinkle with garlic or salt and pat the seasonings into the pastry. If you pierce holes in the pastry it will not puff. Cover the dough with clear plastic and store in the refrigerator until ready to bake.

To make the filling, simmer the chicken pieces, broth, onion, and celery in a covered pot until the chicken is tender, about 30 minutes.

When the chicken is cool enough to handle, remove the skin and bones and cut it into bite-size pieces. Skim the fat off the chicken broth.

Bring 3 cups of the broth to a boil. In a small bowl, mix the flour and butter to form a paste (roux). Stir the paste into the boiling broth and stir constantly for a few minutes until the mixture thickens. Stir in the cream and pepper and simmer for a few more minutes.

Preheat the oven to 425°F.

Place the chicken and vegetables in an 8-cup baking dish or 6 ovenproof serving bowls. Spoon the sauce over the chicken and vegetables. Top with the prepared puff pastry dome. Brush with the beaten egg and place the pastry, brushed-side down over the filling. Press the edges of the pastry firmly against the sides of the dish. Brush egg yolk over the top of the pastry before baking.

Bake for 20 minutes until the pastry is golden brown.

*Hint*

You can also serve this with homemade biscuits or drop biscuits in place of the puff pastry dome.

# CHICKEN NOODLE CASSEROLE

## Ingredients

1 medium onion, chopped

2 tablespoons vegetable oil or water

1 can (49½ ounces) fat-free chicken broth

3 chicken bouillon cubes

3 cloves garlic, pressed

¼ teaspoon thyme

¼ teaspoon pepper

1 teaspoon dill weed

5 sprigs of parsley, snipped

4 carrots, sliced

6 ounces dry wide noodles

3 cups cubed cooked chicken

2 cups nonfat yogurt, at room temperature

2 tablespoons cornstarch

Pinch of sugar, optional

1 cup frozen or canned peas, optional

## Hint

Replace the chicken with 2 cans (6 ounces each) white tuna fish, packed in water and drained, for a fabulous, fat-free tuna noodle casserole.

*M*y beautiful friend, Betty Ann Osborne, prepared this for me as a get-well gift. She had intended for me to dilute it with canned chicken broth, but I loved it thick and creamy and *fat free!*

**Serves 8**

Use a 5-quart pot to cook the onion in the oil or water. Stir the onions until they are soft, about 10 minutes. Add the broth, bouillon, garlic, thyme, pepper, dill, parsley, and carrots.

Cover the pot and bring the mixture to a boil. Reduce the heat and simmer for 20 minutes or until the carrots are soft. Discard the parsley and add the noodles and cook, uncovered, until the noodles are almost soft, 8 to 10 minutes. Add the chicken and keep hot.

Stir the yogurt and cornstarch together and add 1 cup of the hot broth to this mixture. Add the yogurt to the soup and stir until well mixed. Bring the mixture to a boil, stirring constantly.

Add the sugar to smooth out the flavor. Add the peas and serve hot. Garnish with chopped scallions if desired.

# SAUSAGE AND SPINACH FRITTATA

*A* great dish to serve with breakfast or brunch. It can be served cold or hot and is sure to please.

**Serves 4**

Preheat the oven to 350°F. Butter an 8-cup casserole dish and set aside.

Remove and discard the casings from the sausages. Crumble the meat and fry it until it is brown. Drain the cooked sausage on paper towels and pour the remaining fat off the pan.

Add the olive oil and cook the onions and mushrooms until they are soft.

Squeeze the spinach dry and combine the spinach with the eggs, 1 cup grated Parmesan, salt, pepper, and garlic. Stir in the cooked sausage and the onion mixture and stir until well combined.

Spoon the mixture into the prepared pan. Sprinkle the remaining 1/4 cup Parmesan and the mozzarella cheese on top of the casserole and bake for 25 minutes or until the frittata is set.

## Ingredients

2 Italian sausages

2 tablespoons olive oil

1 medium onion, chopped

1/2 pound mushrooms, sliced (2 cups)

1 package (10 ounces) frozen spinach, thawed

6 eggs

1 1/4 cups grated Parmesan cheese

Salt to taste

Pepper to taste

2 cloves garlic, minced

4 ounces mozzarella cheese, grated (1 cup)

# PASTA WITH FOUR CHEESES

## Ingredients

1 pound dry linguine

4 tablespoons (1/2 stick) butter

1/4 pound Italian fontina, cubed (1 cup)

1/4 pound Gorgonzola, cubed (1 cup)

1/4 pound Bel Paese, cubed (1 cup)

1 cup grated Parmesan cheese, fresh if possible

1 cup heavy cream

Freshly ground black pepper to taste

*A*lmost everyone I asked about comfort foods agreed that pasta was one of their first choices. This is an elegant version of macaroni and cheese with lots more taste. Full of comfort and lots of calories!

**Serves 6 to 8**

Cook the pasta until it is firm but tender.

Meanwhile, melt the butter in a saucepan and add the cheeses, stirring constantly until the mixture is well blended and the cheeses are all melted. Add the cream until the sauce is smooth. Do not bring this mixture to a boil. Stir in pepper to taste.

Drain the pasta and place it on a serving platter. Pour the cheese mixture over the pasta and stir until well blended. Sprinkle with a little Parmesan cheese and serve immediately.

# CHEESE MANICOTTI

*A* really delicious, high-fat dinner that is bound to comfort everyone who eats it.

Serves 4

Cook the manicotti in a large pan of lightly salted boiling water for 5 minutes or until almost done but still firm. Drain.

Preheat the oven to 350°F. Butter a 9 × 12-inch baking dish.

Blend the cream cheese until it is smooth and mix in the cottage cheese, mozzarella cheese, eggs, salt, pepper, and nutmeg.

Mix the wine with the spaghetti sauce and pour half of this mixture into the prepared baking dish. Fill each manicotti with about 1/4 cup of the cheese mixture. Use a knife to push the filling through the pasta.

Arrange the filled manicotti on the baking dish and garnish with the mushrooms. Bake 25 minutes or until bubbly. Sprinkle Parmesan cheese over the manicotti and serve hot.

## Ingredients

1 package manicotti (12 pieces)

1 package (8 ounces) cream cheese, at room temperature

1 cup cottage cheese

1/2 pound mozzarella cheese, diced (2 cups)

2 eggs, slightly beaten

1/2 teaspoon salt

Pinch of pepper

1/8 teaspoon nutmeg

1/2 cup red wine

2 cups canned or homemade spaghetti sauce

1 can (3 ounces) sliced mushrooms for garnish

Grated Parmesan cheese

# LASAGNA

## Ingredients

**Lasagna**

1 box (16 ounces) lasagna
  noodles

3 pounds whole milk ricotta
  cheese

2 pounds mozzarella
  cheese, grated

1/2 pound Romano cheese,
  grated

3 eggs, slightly beaten

1/4 teaspoon nutmeg

1/3 cup chopped fresh
  parsley

1/4 teaspoon pepper

1/2 teaspoon salt

1 teaspoon minced garlic

3/4 cup pine nuts, optional

**Tomato sauce**

4 tablespoons minced garlic

1 tablespoon oil

1 teaspoon salt

1/4 teaspoon pepper

1 can (24 ounces) crushed
  tomatoes

6 large fresh basil leaves,
  chopped

*(continues)*

*L*asagna is at the top of the comfort foods list. This recipe is as easy as it gets and is melt-in-your-mouth delicious. Served with the tomato sauce and meatballs on the side, you can please everyone, including vegetarians.

**Serves 6 to 8**

*To make the lasagna:* Preheat the oven to 350°F.

Butter the bottom of a 9 × 14-inch baking dish that is at least 2 inches deep. Prepare the lasagna noodles according to the package directions and cook them al dente. Rinse with cool water so that the noodles do not stick to each other.

Set aside 1/2 cup of the mozzarella and 1/2 cup of the Romano cheese and mix the remaining ingredients together in a separate bowl. Layer the noodles and cheese mixture in the prepared pan, starting with the cheese mixture and ending with the noodles.

Sprinkle the reserved cheese on top of the noodles and cover the pan with foil. Bake for 45 minutes. Remove the foil and cook for an additional 10 minutes or until the cheese starts to bubble and the lasagna is golden brown. Serve with tomato sauce and meatballs.

*To make the tomato sauce:* Sauté the garlic in the oil. Add the salt and pepper and stir in the crushed tomatoes. Simmer for 15 minutes and add the chopped basil leaves. Continue to simmer slowly while preparing the meatballs.

*To make the meatballs:* Mix together all the ingredients except for the sausage and form into small balls. Fry the meatballs with the sliced sausage until well browned. Drain the fat and place the meatballs and sausage in the tomato sauce. (Reserve some tomato sauce without meat for your vegetarian diners.) Serve in a large bowl with the lasagna.

Meatballs

2 pounds ground chuck
12 eggs, lightly beaten
1 teaspoon chopped basil
1 teaspoon chopped parsley
1 teaspoon minced garlic
1/4 teaspoon pepper
1/2 teaspoon salt
1/4 cup bread crumbs
1/4 cup tomato sauce
1 pound hot Italian sausage, sliced

*Hint*

Instead of lasagna noodles, use the crepe recipe from the cheese blintzes (page 261) and double the recipe.

# MACARONI AND CHEESE

## Ingredients

½ cup (1 stick) butter

½ cup flour

4 cups milk or light cream

4 eggs, well beaten

Salt

Pepper

Nutmeg or cardamom

2 cups ricotta cheese
   (16 ounces)

1 pound sharp Cheddar
   cheese, grated (4 cups)

1 pound dry macaroni or
   fancy pasta curls

*T*here are some impressively fancy names for this pasta dish but the old-fashioned, thick and creamy stuff is the most comforting. Serve this with a Caesar salad (page 91).

**Serves 8**

Melt the butter in a large saucepan. Whisk in the flour using a wire whisk. In another pan, bring the milk to a boil and slowly add the flour mixture, stirring constantly.

When the mixture has thickened, remove it from the heat and allow it to cool slightly. Add the beaten eggs, seasonings, and ricotta cheese. Add the Cheddar cheese.

Preheat the oven to 350°F. Butter an 8-cup casserole dish.

Cook the pasta according to the package directions. Drain and stir in the sauce using a fork. Pour the macaroni and cheese into the prepared casserole. Bake for 20 minutes or until thoroughly heated.

# FETTUCINE ALFREDO

*C*reamy and delicious as a main dish with a salad, or as a side dish with a roast. This is yummy!

**Serves 4**

Cook the noodles according to the package directions. Drain the noodles. Place the noodles on a serving platter.

While the pasta is cooking, prepare the sauce. Over very low heat, whisk the cream and egg yolk together until well mixed and warm. *Do not boil*. Toss the noodles gently with the cheese, butter, and cream mixture. Season to taste with salt and pepper and add nutmeg if desired.

## Ingredients

1 pound dry fettucine noodles

1 cup heavy cream

1 egg yolk

2 cups freshly grated Parmesan cheese

1 cup (2 sticks) butter, at room temperature

White pepper

Salt

Nutmeg, optional

# SPAGHETTI AND MEATBALLS

## Ingredients

1 egg, beaten

¼ cup milk

1 slice soft white bread

⅓ cup grated Parmesan cheese

½ teaspoon salt

1 teaspoon pepper

1 teaspoon dried oregano, crushed

1 pound ground beef

½ pound ground pork

1 onion, chopped

3 cloves garlic, minced

2 tablespoons olive oil

1 can (18 ounces) Italian plum tomatoes, chopped with juice

2 cans (6 ounces each) tomato paste

½ cup water

1 tablespoon sugar

1 teaspoon salt

2 bay leaves

8 ounces spaghetti, cooked according to package directions

Grated Parmesan or Cheddar cheese, optional

*A* favorite comfort food. Simmer the sauce slowly and let the aroma permeate the house. Your family will go mad with desire. Serve it with a Caesar salad (page 91) and garlic bread—who could ask for anything more?

**Serves 6**

Combine the egg and milk and crumble in the bread. Add ⅓ cup Parmesan, salt, ½ teaspoon pepper, and ½ teaspoon oregano. Add the ground beef and ground pork and mix well. Wet your hands. This will make it easier to shape the meatballs. Make the meatballs as small or as big as you like.

In a deep saucepan, cook the onions and garlic in olive oil until the onions are transparent. Remove the onions and brown the meatballs, turning them often. Drain off any excess fat.

Stir in the undrained tomatoes, tomato paste, water, sugar, ½ teaspoon oregano, salt, ½ teaspoon pepper, and bay leaves.

Cover the pot and simmer for at least 1 hour, stirring occasionally.

Remove the bay leaves before serving over hot spaghetti. Pass the grated cheese.

## Hint

If you want a spicier sauce, add hot pepper flakes or hot sauce to taste. You can eliminate the ground pork and add chunks of hot Italian sausage or use ground chicken or turkey browned with the beef.

# PASTA PRIMAVERA

## Ingredients

12 ounces dry fettuccine or
    spaghetti
3 tablespoons butter
1 small eggplant, peeled
    and cut into thin strips
2 carrots, cut into thin
    strips
3 cloves garlic, minced
1/2 pound fresh mushrooms,
    sliced thin (2 cups)
2 ounces prosciutto ham,
    cut into thin strips
2 small zucchini, shredded
1 large tomato, peeled and
    cut into thin wedges
1/2 cup heavy cream
1/4 cup chopped fresh basil
Salt
Ground black pepper
1/2 cup grated Parmesan
    cheese

This is a great comfort food. Primavera means springtime in Italian and you can use any fresh vegetables you like.

**Serves 6**

Cook the pasta until tender but firm.

While the pasta is cooking, prepare the sauce. In a large saucepan, melt the butter and sauté the eggplant, carrots, garlic, and mushrooms for 1 minute. Add the ham and zucchini and sauté for 1 more minute. Add the tomato and cream and simmer the mixture for 5 minutes. Stir in the basil and season to taste with salt and pepper.

Drain the pasta and place on a serving platter. Mix the sauce and pasta. Sprinkle grated Parmesan on top of the pasta and serve immediately.

# BEEF BRISKET IN BEER

$\mathcal{T}$his is my family's favorite comfort food. It should be sliced thin and served hot with baked or mashed potatoes. It is a little spicy and full of flavor. The gravy, which is dark and thick, makes marvelous onion soup. Just add 1 cup chicken broth to each cup of gravy when serving it as soup.

**Serves 8 hearty eaters**

Preheat the oven to 350°F.

Brown the onions in the olive oil until they are transparent. Remove the onions from the pan and place in the bottom of a large roasting pan with a cover.

Slowly brown the brisket in the frying pan. Sprinkle the meat with salt, pepper, and paprika and cook until dark golden brown on both sides. Remove the meat from the pan and place on top of the cooked onions.

Add the garlic, bay leaves, soy sauce, brown sugar, and Worcestershire sauce. Pour the beer on top of everything.

Cover the baking pan and bake it for 2 hours or until the beef is almost tender.

Remove the beef and allow it to cool sufficiently to slice it very thin. Return the beef to the pan and add the sliced mushrooms. Bake for an additional 30 minutes. Remove the bay leaves and serve hot.

## Ingredients

8 cups onions, thinly sliced

4 tablespoons olive oil

5 pounds of lean beef brisket

1 tablespoon salt

1 tablespoon freshly ground pepper

2 tablespoons paprika

4 cloves garlic, minced

8 bay leaves

3 tablespoons soy sauce

1/2 cup firmly packed brown sugar

1 tablespoon Worcester-shire sauce

1 pint beer (2 cups)

1/2 pound mushrooms, thinly sliced (2 cups)

## Hint

This is another dish that should be prepared at least 1 or 2 days in advance and refrigerated. This allows the flavors to blend and the congealed fat to be skimmed off the beef.

# BARBECUED BABY BACK RIBS

## Ingredients

5 to 6 pounds of well
trimmed baby back ribs

2 jars (12 ounces each) chili
sauce

1 tablespoon salt

1 teaspoon ground pepper

1 tablespoon minced garlic

8 cups chopped onions

3 cups wine vinegar

4 cups water

6 bay leaves

10 drops of hot sauce

1 cup firmly packed dark
brown sugar

*A*s a teenager growing up in Detroit, I was sure that spare ribs were the most comforting food available, anywhere. I now consider this recipe the very best! My daughter Lisa requests these for her birthday.

**Serves 6**

Broil the ribs on both sides and place in a large baking dish. Pour off the fat left in the broiler pan. Arrange the ribs so that they do not overlap each other. Use two large baking pans if necessary.

Pour the chili sauce into a large pot. Add the scrapings from the broiler pan after you have discarded the fat. Add the salt, pepper, garlic, onions, vinegar, water, bay leaves, hot sauce, and brown sugar.

Bring the sauce to a boil and simmer for 1 hour. When the sauce is almost done, preheat the oven to 400°F.

Pour the sauce over the ribs and place the pans in the hot oven. Bake for 1 hour or until the ribs are browned. Turn the ribs using tongs and cook for an additional 20 minutes until the ribs are brown on both sides.

I like to make the ribs 24 hours in advance of serving them. I refrigerate the ribs and allow them to cool completely. At that point, I remove any congealed fat that comes to the surface, as well as the bay leaves.

Reheat the ribs and serve with crusty baked potatoes or garlic mashed potatoes (page 204).

# STANDING RIB ROAST

## Ingredients

1 rib roast, 2 to 4 ribs, well
   trimmed
4 tablespoons garlic powder
   or minced garlic
2 teaspoons salt
1 teaspoon freshly ground
   pepper

*A*bsolutely perfect—the beef should be pink
on the inside and crispy brown on the outside.

**Two ribs serve 4, three ribs serve 6 to 8**

About 3 hours before you plan to serve your
dinner, preheat the oven to 400°F. Remember it
takes about 10 minutes for the oven to reach the
desired heat.

Place the rib roast in a roasting pan. If you
have a meat rack, place the meat on the rack in
the pan. In a small bowl, mix together the garlic,
salt, and pepper. Rub the roast with the garlic
mixture. Place the roast in the heated oven and
allow it to bake for 1 hour. At the end of that
hour, turn off the heat and keep the oven door
shut until serving time. Your roast can be reheated for 15 minutes if desired and served hot.

# BEEF CURRY

Serve this deliciously different beef dish with chutney, chopped nuts, raisins, and coconut.

Serves 4

Heat the oil in a saucepan and cook the onion until it is transparent. Add the curry powder.

Stir in the beef, chopped apples, 3/4 cup of the water, the beef bouillon, raisins, and salt. Season to taste with extra curry or salt.

Blend together the flour and remaining 1/4 cup water. When the curry starts to bubble, stir in the flour mixture until the curry thickens.

Serve hot over rice.

## Ingredients

1 tablespoon vegetable oil

1/2 cup finely chopped onion

2 teaspoons curry powder

3 cups cooked beef, cut into cubes or strips

2 small apples, peeled, cored, and chopped

1 cup water

1 teaspoon instant beef bouillon granules

1/2 cup raisins

1/2 teaspoon salt

1 tablespoon flour

Hot cooked rice

# THE PERFECT STEAK

¹/₄ cup mustard sauce
(page 225)
4 sirloin strip steaks, 12 to
14 ounces each
3 tablespoons cracked black
peppercorns
¹/₂ cup clarified butter
(page 228)

**Cognac mustard sauce**

2 tablespoons butter
1 tablespoon chives
¹/₄ cup cognac
¹/₂ cup mustard sauce
(page 225)
¹/₄ cup coffee cream

*M*eat and potato people will tell you that steak is their idea of comfort food. The cognac mustard sauce is what makes the steak perfect. It is truly worth the effort.

**Serves 4; makes 1 cup of sauce**

Spread 1 teaspoon mustard sauce on one side of each steak and press 1 teaspoon of cracked black peppercorns into the meat. Turn the steaks and repeat this process. Cover and refrigerate the steaks for at least 8 hours or overnight.

Remember the reason to clarify the butter is so that you can heat it to a high temperature without having it smoke. Use a heavy skillet and melt the butter. Pan-fry the steaks, turning only once until they reach the desired doneness.

*Rare:* 4 to 5 minutes each side

*Medium rare:* 5 to 6 minutes each side

*Medium:* 6 to 7 minutes each side

While the steaks are cooking, prepare the cognac mustard sauce. Melt the butter in a frying pan and cook the chives for 1 minute. Add the cognac and boil for 2 minutes to let the alcohol evaporate. Remove the pan from the heat.

Add the mustard sauce and cream and stir until smooth.

Place over very low heat until mixture starts to bubble. Serve over steaks immediately.

# MEATLOAF

*T*his quick and easy recipe for a classic comfort food comes from Sue Drucker.

**Serves 6**

2 pounds ground beef,
   turkey, or chicken
1 package onion soup mix
2 eggs
1/3 cup catsup
1 1/3 cups uncooked oatmeal
3/4 cup water
1/2 cup finely chopped
   green bell pepper,
   optional
1 tablespoon minced garlic,
   optional

Preheat the oven to 350°F.

Combine all ingredients in a large bowl. Knead well with fingers to combine. Shape and place in a loaf pan. Bake for 1 hour.

# SCHNITZEL

## Ingredients

1 pound veal or pork cutlets
Salt and pepper
1/2 cup flour
2 eggs, beaten
1 cup bread crumbs
Oil

*T*his recipe is the comfort food of my favorite nurse, Liz Warren, who brought the recipe with her from Germany. You can substitute pork for the veal if you prefer.

**Serves 3 to 4**

Pound the chops as thin as possible and sprinkle with salt and pepper. Coat each cutlet with flour, then dip the meat in the eggs, and then in the bread crumbs. Make sure that each cutlet is well coated.

Heat oil in a heavy skillet and cook the meat until it is golden brown, about 2 minutes on each side. Enjoy!

*For pepper schnitzel:* Sauté 1 chopped onion and 1 chopped green pepper and serve on top of the meat.

*For cream schnitzel:* After the meat has been well browned, remove it from the pan. Pour off the excess fat and add 1/2 cup of sour cream. Heat gently making sure that you scrape any brown bits from the bottom of the pan. Pour over the cutlets and serve.

*For hunter schnitzel:* Sauté 1/2 pound (2 cups) of sliced mushrooms together with 1 chopped onion. Stir in 1 tablespoon of flour and slowly add 1/2 cup of white wine. Bring the mixture to a boil, stirring constantly, and boil for 1 minute. Top the meat with this sauce.

# RACK OF LAMB

Some of you prefer eating lamb to counting sheep. This is an elegant way to serve lamb, especially if you can find those cute little paper caps that fit over the top of the lamb bones. Serve this with mint jelly, or the Greek way, with lemon. Ask your butcher to remove the fat from the lamb and "French" the rib bones.

Serves 4

Mix together the oil, basil, thyme, garlic, salt, and pepper to make a marinade.

Brush the lamb thoroughly with the marinade and place the lamb in a shallow roasting pan. Cover and marinate in the refrigerator for 24 hours or overnight.

Preheat the oven to 350°F. Place the lamb on a rack and cook for 45 minutes or until the meat reaches 140°F using a meat thermometer.

Remove the roast from the oven, cover with foil and let it stand for 10 minutes before serving by slicing between each rib blade with a sharp knife.

## Ingredients

½ cup olive oil

1 tablespoon chopped fresh basil, or 1 teaspoon dried

1 teaspoon chopped fresh thyme, or 1 teaspoon dried

1 teaspoon minced garlic

1 teaspoon salt

1 teaspoon ground pepper

2 pounds rack of lamb

# MOUSSAKA

## Ingredients

2 large eggplants, peeled
　　and sliced crosswise

1½ cups flour

½ cup olive oil

1 pound bulk sausage meat

1 large onion, chopped

2 pounds lean ground lamb
　　or beef

1 teaspoon oregano,
　　crumbled

3 cloves garlic, minced

1 cup tomato purée or
　　paste

½ teaspoon salt

½ teaspoon pepper

1 cup red wine

1 bunch fresh spinach,
　　washed and dried

½ pound fresh mushrooms,
　　sliced (2 cups)

4 tablespoons (½ stick)
　　butter

2 cups light cream

Pinch of nutmeg

1 cup ricotta cheese

*I* love this recipe for moussaka. It does require
effort, but if you love moussaka, you'll adore this.

**Serves 6**

Sprinkle the sliced eggplant with salt and set
it on a cookie sheet covered with paper towels so
that the slices do not overlap. Set aside for 30
minutes.

Place 1 cup of flour in a plastic bag and shake
a few slices of eggplant at a time in the flour.
Heat ¼ cup olive oil in a large frying pan and
lightly sauté the eggplant slices. Set them aside.

Brown the sausage meat in the same skillet
and drain off the fat except for 2 tablespoons.
Set the sausage meat aside.

In the same skillet, sauté the onion in the
sausage fat. Add the sausage meat.

In another skillet, brown the lamb in ¼ cup
oil and season with oregano. Add to the sausage
mixture.

Sauté the garlic until it is golden and add the tomato purée, salt, and pepper. Mix well. Add the wine and all the cooked meats. Simmer, uncovered until almost all the liquid is absorbed.

Preheat the oven to 400°F.

Butter a 5-quart casserole or baking dish and layer the eggplant at the bottom. Cover with a layer of the meat mixture. Add the spinach leaves and top with the mushrooms.

Melt the butter in a saucepan and stir in the remaining ½ cup of flour. Cook, stirring constantly, until thick. Slowly add the cream and cook until thick and smooth. Season with nutmeg and pour over the casserole. Top with ricotta cheese and bake, covered, for 45 minutes. Uncover and bake an additional 15 minutes or until golden brown.

# BEEF BOURGUIGNON

## Ingredients

¼ pound salt pork, diced

¼ cup cognac

¼ cup chopped parsley

¾ teaspoon freshly ground
   black pepper

½ cup flour

1 teaspoon salt

Dash of cayenne pepper

3 pounds bottom round or
   better beef, cubed

6 tablespoons plus
   1 teaspoon butter

2 large onions, chopped

2 cups beef broth

1½ cups Burgundy or red
   wine

½ teaspoon thyme

½ teaspoon dried
   marjoram

1 pound fresh mushrooms,
   sliced (4 cups)

16 small white onions,
   peeled, or canned

2 large potatoes, diced

*N*o matter how you pronounce this, it's a fancy name for beef stew. But, it is elegant enough to serve at your fanciest party. The combination of flavors is perfect and since it should be prepared in advance, it's easy to serve with rice and a good red wine.

**Serves 8**

Marinate the salt pork in cognac, parsley, and ¼ teaspoon black pepper for several hours. Mix together the flour, salt, ½ teaspoon black pepper, and cayenne in a plastic bag. Shake the beef in the seasoned flour. Melt 4 tablespoons of the butter in a saucepan and thoroughly brown the meat.

Preheat the oven to 375°F. Place the cooked beef and onions in a 3-quart casserole or a lovely big baking dish that has a tight fitting lid, or use foil and create your own lid.

Drain the salt pork and save the liquid. Brown the salt pork in 1 teaspoon of the butter. Add to the beef.

Pour the marinade in the skillet with ¼ cup of the beef broth. Scrape the crispies off the bottom of the pan and pour everything over the meat.

Add the wine, thyme, and marjoram with enough broth to cover the meat. Cover the casserole and bake for 2 hours.

Sauté the mushrooms in 2 tablespoons of butter until they are soft. If you are using fresh tiny onions, peel them and parboil them for a few minutes. If you are using canned onions, drain them.

Add the mushrooms, onions, and diced potatoes to the meat and continue cooking for 1 additional hour. Add more wine or beef broth if needed.

*Hint*

If you like a spicy flavor, add 1 teaspoon minced garlic and a pinch of cayenne pepper when you add the beef broth.

# GLAZED CORNED BEEF

## Ingredients

1 large corned beef brisket
(6 to 10 pounds), or 2
smaller briskets
12 peppercorns, lightly
crushed
3 bay leaves
1 large onion, quartered
6 whole cloves
3 cloves garlic, mashed

### Glaze

3/4 cup firmly packed dark
brown sugar
1 tablespoon dry mustard
1 tablespoon cider vinegar

*M*aybe the only thing better than corned beef is glazed corned beef. It is unforgettable. Ask the butcher to help you select the leanest brisket.

**Serves 8 to 10**

Place the corned beef in a large pot with the seasonings and enough water to cover the meat. Bring to a boil and skim off any foam that rises to the top of the water.

Cover the pot, lower the heat, and simmer for 3 hours or until the meat is tender.

Allow the brisket to cool in the water in which it has been cooked for 30 minutes.

Preheat the oven to 300°F.

Combine the glaze ingredients. Place the corned beef on a roasting pan and coat with the glaze. Bake uncovered for 1 hour, basting occasionally.

# CHICKEN-FRIED STEAK

*This* came in second as everyone's favorite comfort food, especially served with garlic mashed potatoes (page 204).

**Serves 4**

## Ingredients

2 pounds of round steak, cut ½ inch thick, tenderized by the butcher
2 cups buttermilk
2 cups flour or bread crumbs
1 teaspoon salt
1 teaspoon granulated garlic
1 teaspoon pepper
Canola oil for frying

Cut the steak into serving-size pieces. Soak the beef in buttermilk, cover, and allow to marinate in the refrigerator for 2 hours or overnight.

Mix together the flour, salt, garlic, and pepper and place the mixture in a large flat plate or pie pan. Coat the steak, 1 piece at a time, in the flour mixture. Heat the oil in a large pan and fry the beef until golden brown on both sides. Serve with pan gravy (page 136), if desired.

# CHICKEN-FRIED PORK CHOPS

## Ingredients

1 egg, well beaten
1 tablespoon milk
8 pork chops, 1/2 inch thick
1 cup dry bread crumbs
2 tablespoons vegetable oil
1/2 teaspoon salt
1/4 teaspoon pepper
1/2 teaspoon garlic powder
1/4 cup water or white wine

*O*h, yes, these are the real thing. Moist on the inside, crunchy on the outside.

**Serves 4**

Mix the egg and milk together. Dip the meat in this mixture and then in the crumbs. Repeat to make sure the chops are well coated.

Heat the oil in a frying pan and brown the chops on both sides. Season with salt, pepper, and garlic powder.

Add the water or white wine to the chops and cover the pan. Reduce heat to low and simmer for 15 minutes. Remove the cover and lift the chops to prevent them from sticking. Cook an additional 10 to 15 minutes or until the chops are crisp.

# ROAST PORK

*R*oast pork got a lot of mention as a comfort food. Try this marinated roast served with applesauce.

**Serves 4**

Split the roast lengthwise. Combine the remaining ingredients in a large bowl and add the meat.

Cover and marinate overnight, turning the roast occasionally.

Preheat the oven to 375°F. Drain the meat and roast it for about 1½ hours or until a meat thermometer registers 175°F.

## Ingredients

1 boned pork loin
   (3 pounds)
1 large onion, chopped
6 cloves garlic, crushed
½ cup soy sauce
¼ cup cider vinegar
2 tablespoons oil
1 tablespoon firmly packed
   brown sugar
1 teaspoon curry powder
1 teaspoon oregano
½ teaspoon pepper

# PIZZA

## Ingredients

### Crust

2 packages (¼ ounce each)
   dry yeast
1¼ cups warm water
   (110° to 115°F)
1 teaspoon sugar
3½ cups flour, high gluten
   if available
1 teaspoon salt
¼ cup vegetable oil

### Sauce

3 tablespoons olive oil
1 large onion, finely
   chopped
2 tablespoons minced garlic
1 can (28 ounces) tomatoes,
   undrained, chopped
1 can (6 ounces) tomato
   paste
1 bay leaf
1 tablespoon oregano
1 tablespoon sugar
1 tablespoon salt
¼ teaspoon pepper

*P*izza is probably the number one comfort food choice for kids and adults alike. It's relatively simple to make and you can buy a prepared crust or make your own. Homemade crust will make your kitchen smell like heaven. You can use the traditional cheese and pepperoni or you can try an assortment of sausages, cheeses, mushrooms, onions, peppers, ground beef, or other sliced meats.

**Makes 2 (14-inch) pizzas, about 4 servings**

To make the crust, dissolve the yeast in the warm water and add the sugar. In a large bowl combine the flour, salt, and oil. Add the yeast mixture and stir to combine all the ingredients. Knead the dough until it is satiny and smooth on a floured cloth or board, about 5 minutes.

Place the dough in a greased bowl, cover, and put it in a warm place. Let the dough double in size, about 1 hour. Punch down the dough and knead it a little. Divide the dough into 2 pieces and roll out the dough into 2 (14-inch) rounds, to fit into 2 pizza pans or on baking sheets.

While the dough is rising, make the sauce in a large pot. Heat the oil and sauté the chopped onion and garlic until the onion is transparent. Add the remaining sauce ingredients and bring the mixture to a boil. Lower the heat and simmer uncovered for at least 1 hour, stirring occasionally.

Preheat the oven to 500°F. Cover the pizza dough with the sauce and add any combination of cheeses, meats, or vegetables you like. Bake for 10 to 15 minutes or until the crust is evenly browned.

# DEEP-DISH PIZZA

**Dough**

1 package (¼ ounce) dry
    yeast

1 cup warm water
    (110° to 115°F)

1 tablespoon sugar

1 teaspoon salt

2 tablespoons oil

2½ to 3 cups flour

**Meat sauce**

1 pound Italian sausage

½ cup chopped onion

1 tablespoon minced garlic

1 can (16 ounces) tomatoes,
    chopped, undrained

1 can (6 ounces) tomato
    paste

½ pound mushrooms,
    sliced (2 cups)

1 teaspoon oregano

1 teaspoon salt

¼ teaspoon pepper

*(continues)*

You will need a special pan for this. It's worth the effort and it is better than the pizza made at the local pizza parlor.

**Makes 1 deep-dish pizza, about 6 servings**

To make the crust, dissolve the yeast in the warm water. Add the sugar, salt, and oil. Mix well. Gradually add flour to this mixture until a stiff dough has been formed. Knead on a floured surface until the dough is smooth and shiny, about 5 minutes. Place the dough in a greased bowl and cover it with a towel. Allow it to rise in a warm place until it has doubled in bulk, about 1 hour.

Brown the meat in a large frying pan with the garlic and onion. Drain the fat. Add the remaining sauce ingredients and bring to a boil. Lower heat and simmer for 30 minutes, uncovered. Cool the sauce.

Combine all the cheese filling ingredients until well mixed, and set aside.

In another bowl, combine all the topping ingredients and set aside.

Preheat the oven at 400°F.

Roll out half the dough on a floured surface and place into a deep-dish pizza pan or onto a 11 × 17-inch jelly roll pan with sides. With your fingertips, press the dough over the bottom and up the sides of the pan. Spread the cheese filling on the dough. Roll out the remaining dough and place it over the cheese filling. Cover this dough with the meat sauce.

Bake for 15 minutes. Sprinkle the pizza with the topping mixture and bake an additional 15 minutes or until the pizza is golden brown.

### Cheese filling

1 pound ricotta cheese

1/2 pound mozzarella cheese, grated (2 cups)

2 eggs, beaten

1/2 teaspoon salt

### Topping

1/2 pound mozzarella cheese, grated (2 cups)

1/2 teaspoon oregano

1/2 cup grated Parmesan cheese

# CALZONE

## Ingredients

2 loaves (1 pound each)
  frozen bread dough,
  thawed

1 pound prosciutto ham,
  thinly sliced

1 pint ricotta cheese
  (16 ounces)

2 cloves garlic, crushed

4 ounces blue cheese,
  crumbled

1/2 cup chopped fresh basil

2 tablespoons chopped
  fresh oregano

1 can (14 ounces) Italian
  plum tomatoes

1 egg, well beaten with
  2 tablespoons water

Calzone is really a pizza that has been folded in half and baked like a turnover. In this recipe, the calzone is shaped like a pizza with a top and bottom crust. This version is simplified by using frozen bread dough. If you have a bread machine, you can make your own.

**Serves 4**

Preheat the oven to 350°F.

Roll the defrosted bread dough into 2 (12-inch) rounds. Place one round of dough on a lightly oiled cookie sheet and sprinkle on the ham, ricotta cheese, and garlic. Leave 1 inch plain around the edges of the dough circle.

Sprinkle on the crumbled blue cheese, basil, and oregano. Drain the tomatoes and chop them into pieces.

Spoon the tomatoes over the filling. Brush the edges of the dough with water and place the second 12-inch round of bread dough on top of the filling. Press the edges together. Use the tines of a fork to help seal the edges.

Cut several slits in the top of the calzone to allow steam to escape while baking. Brush the top with the egg-water mixture. Bake for 45 minutes or until the calzone is golden brown and sounds hollow when tapped.

# FRIED SHRIMP

*T*here is no way that you can make enough of this to comfort everyone. This coating is light and crunchy and the shrimp are cooked to pink perfection.

**Serves 4**

## Ingredients

2 pounds large uncooked
    shrimp, peeled and
    deveined
1/4 cup flour
3/4 cup water or stale beer
1 egg, slightly beaten
1 tablespoon sugar
1/2 teaspoon salt
Peanut oil for deep-frying

Butterfly the cleaned shrimp so that they will look larger: Hold so that the underside is up. Slice down its length, almost to the vein, to form the hinge. Spread and flatten to form the butterfly shape.

Make a batter by mixing together the flour, water, egg, sugar, and salt.

Use a deep fryer and heat the oil to 375°F. Dip the shrimp in batter and fry until golden brown. Drain on paper towels.

# SMOKED SALMON TART

## Ingredients

1 unbaked 9-inch pie shell
1 egg white, lightly beaten
$1/2$ pound smoked salmon,
    flaked or chopped
1 cup grated Swiss cheese
4 eggs
$1 1/4$ cups half-and-half
1 tablespoon chopped fresh
    dill or 1 teaspoon dried
    dill weed
$1/2$ teaspoon salt
$1/4$ teaspoon pepper
Caviar for garnish, optional

*I*mpressive to serve and simple to prepare. If you live in an area where the end pieces of smoked salmon are available, use these inexpensive pieces.

**Serves 4 as a main dish, 8 as an appetizer**

Preheat the oven to 400°F.

Brush the pie shell with the egg white and bake for 5 minutes. Let the shell cool a little.

Combine the remaining ingredients except for the caviar garnish. Pour into the prepared crust and bake for 15 minutes.

Reduce the oven temperature to 350°F and continue baking the tart for an additional 15 minutes or until the top of the tart is golden brown. Garnish with the caviar.

# LOX AND EGGS

*T*his is just like the lox and eggs you can order at the Carnegie Deli in New York City. The wait people there are rude enough to be entertaining, but this mountain of deliciousness can drive away the demons.

**Serves 2**

Melt the butter in a large frying pan. Cook the onion until it is transparent. Add the salmon and cook uncovered for 1 minute.

Mix together the eggs and milk and add to the onions and lox. Cook on high until the omelet is set and then stir for about 3 minutes until the eggs are cooked.

## Ingredients

2 tablespoons butter

1 small onion, diced

2 ounces smoked salmon or gravlox, chopped

6 eggs

6 tablespoons milk or cream

# SWEET AND
# SOUR SHRIMP

## Ingredients

2 pounds large raw shrimp,
    peeled

2 tablespoons red wine

1/4 cup soy sauce

1/4 cup flour

2 tablespoons cornstarch

Oil for deep frying

1 onion, quartered

3 green bell peppers,
    quartered

1 carrot, cut into wedges
    and boiled for 8 minutes

4 ounces water chestnuts

1/2 can pineapple chunks,
    drained

5 tablespoons oil

1/4 cup sugar

1/2 cup soy sauce

2 tablespoons wine

1/4 cup vinegar

1/2 cup tomato sauce

2 tablespoons cornstarch
    mixed with 1/2 cup water

I personally don't know anyone who does not love shrimp. This is delicious served over hot rice.

**Serves 4**

First assemble all the ingredients including the deep fryer. Remember you can reuse peanut and canola oil if you strain the oil after it is used and keep it in a tightly sealed container between uses.

Coat the shrimp with a mixture of the red wine, soy sauce, flour, and 2 tablespoons cornstarch. Deep-fry the shrimp in hot oil (375°F) for 2 minutes and place on paper towels to drain.

Sauté the onion, green peppers, carrot, water chestnuts, and pineapple in 5 tablespoons of vegetable oil until the onions and peppers are soft, about 5 minutes.

Mix together the sugar, soy sauce, wine, vinegar, and tomato sauce and add to the sautéed vegetables. When the mixture boils, add the cornstarch mixture and stir until the thickened. Add the shrimp, mix well, and serve hot over rice.

# PAELLA

*T*his is labor intensive but worth the effort. I once prepared this for a party at which I really wanted to impress a young man. As we rushed him to the emergency room of a local hospital he admitted that he was allergic to shellfish! I still love paella. A real show stopper served in an iron pot or huge ceramic baking pan.

**Serves 4 to 6**

Heat 2 tablespoons oil in a large frying pan. Fry the chicken pieces, sausage, and pork in the oil until brown, about 15 minutes. Add the green pepper, fish, and shrimp and fry for an additional 5 minutes. Use more olive oil if necessary. Add the rice and mix everything together. Add the clams and keep the mixture on low heat. Cover the pot and simmer until clams open, about 10 minutes.

Use a separate saucepan. Heat 2 tablespoons olive oil. Add the tomatoes, onion, garlic, pimiento, parsley, cinnamon, paprika, bay leaves, salt, saffron, and 2 cups boiling water. Mix thoroughly. Add the peas and cook over medium heat for 10 minutes.

Mix all the ingredients together and cook, covered, for 10 minutes or until the rice is soft and all the liquid has been absorbed by the rice.

The fish will flake and the saffron will turn the mixture yellow. Serve hot.

## Ingredients

4 tablespoons olive oil
1/2 pound chicken, cut into bite-size pieces
1/2 pound sausage, cut into bite-size pieces
1/2 pound pork cutlets, cut into bite-size pieces
1 green bell pepper, chopped
1/2 pound white fish fillets
1 pound shrimp, in the shell
1 cup rice
1 dozen small clams in the shell, scrubbed
2 large tomatoes, diced
1 onion, diced
4 cloves garlic, crushed
Pimientos, optional but pretty
Parsley
1/4 teaspoon cinnamon
1 teaspoon paprika
2 bay leaves
1 teaspoon salt
1/4 teaspoon saffron
2 cups boiling water
1/2 pound frozen peas

# TUNA NOODLE CASSEROLE

## Ingredients

1 package (1½ ounces)
cheese sauce mix

½ cup milk or cream

1 cup cottage cheese

½ package (10-ounce size)
frozen peas

1 can (6½ ounces) white
chunk tuna, drained and
flaked

4 ounces egg noodles,
cooked and drained

½ cup crushed potato chips

½ cup grated Cheddar
cheese

*L*ots of people choose this as their comfort food—they tell me that they crave it. Use a cheese sauce mix to make preparation easy.

**Serves 4**

Preheat the oven to 375°F. Butter a 6-cup casserole.

In a large saucepan, blend together the cheese sauce mix and the milk until smooth. Add the cottage cheese and cook, stirring constantly, until the mixture boils. Add the peas to the sauce and cook until the peas are tender and the sauce is thick, about 5 minutes.

Fold in the tuna and the noodles. Spoon the mixture into the baking dish. Top with crushed potato chips and grated Cheddar cheese.

Bake 15 to 20 minutes or until bubbly.

# TUNA CROQUETTES

*T*his is an old-fashioned comfort food from my childhood. There is nothing as good as a perfectly fried croquette.

**Serves 4**

Melt the butter in a saucepan. Stir in the flour and add the milk. Cook until the sauce thickens. Add the onion, lemon juice, salt, pepper, and paprika. Stir in the tuna.

Cover the mixture with plastic wrap and refrigerate at least 3 hours or overnight.

Moisten your hands and shape the tuna mixture into 8 cone shapes—about ¼ cup of mixture for each cone. Or, shape the mixture into patties if you prefer.

Coat each cone or patty with bread crumbs. Then, dip the cone into the egg-water mixture and dip in bread crumbs again until well coated.

Heat vegetable oil to 350°F and fry the croquettes for 2 minutes or until they turn golden brown on both sides. While the croquettes are cooking, prepare the peas with cream sauce according to the package directions.

Drain the croquettes on paper towels and serve with the peas.

## Ingredients

3 tablespoons butter
¼ cup flour
⅔ cup milk
2 tablespoons grated onion
2 teaspoons lemon juice
¼ teaspoon salt
Pinch of pepper
Pinch of paprika
2 cans (6 ounces each) tuna, drained and flaked
⅔ cup bread crumbs
1 egg, beaten with 2 tablespoons water
1 package (8 ounces) peas with cream sauce

# ON THE SIDE

---

$S$ome of us can make a meal of side dishes. No matter how you serve or eat the following recipes, enjoy. That is the true goal in life.

# FRITTERS

$\mathcal{T}$his tops the comfort food list as far as I am concerned. I'm not sure who said, "Everything I love is either fattening, illegal, or immoral," but everything I love is fried.

This is an old-fashioned treat, and while it is simple and memorable, it does require deep-fat frying.

I've got a tiny fryer. I save the oil after each use, strain it into a jar, and store it tightly sealed so that I can reuse it. I've been told that lard and bear fat make the best frying agents. I'll never know because I use canola oil.

**Serves 6**

## Ingredients

1 can of corn, *or* 2 cups of chopped, peeled tart apples, *or* 2 bananas, sliced
1 1/2 cups flour
1 tablespoon baking powder
Pinch of salt
1 egg, beaten
1 cup milk

Drain the corn. Mix the flour and baking powder together and add the salt, egg, and milk and mix until just moistened. Stir in the corn.

Heat the oil to 375°F, using a thermometer. Drop the batter into hot oil by the tablespoonful. Fry for a few minutes until golden brown.

Drain on paper towels and serve.

# SPÄTZLE (GERMAN DROP DUMPLINGS)

## Ingredients

3 cups flour

1 teaspoon salt

1/4 teaspoon baking powder

1/4 teaspoon nutmeg

4 eggs, well beaten

1 cup milk

2 tablespoons (1/4 stick)
    butter, melted

2 tablespoons chopped
    parsley

Salt and pepper to taste

These light and fluffy little dumplings are wonderful with stew or meat dishes. They are unusual and fun to serve.

Serves 4

Mix together the flour, salt, baking powder, and nutmeg. Stir in the eggs and slowly add enough milk to make a smooth, but not stiff, dough.

This is the interesting part: Boil 2 quarts of lightly salted water. When the water is boiling, force the flour mixture through a colander with large holes, into the water.

Boil for 5 minutes or until the dumplings float on top of the water. Drain and transfer to a warm serving bowl.

Toss with butter and parsley and season with salt and pepper.

# POLENTA DUMPLINGS

*P*olenta, which is corn meal mush, is becoming increasingly popular. You can prepare it according to the package directions and serve it as mush with a dab of butter, or chill, slice, and fry it and serve it with an entrée.

**Makes 8 dumplings**

Combine the water, polenta, salt, and pepper in a saucepan and cook, stirring constantly, until the mixture bubbles. Cook for 1 more minute.

Remove from heat and cool slightly. Add the egg and beat until smooth. Add the flour and baking powder and mix until smooth.

In a large pot, boil water or broth. Drop the dumplings by the heaping teaspoonful into the boiling liquid. Cover and simmer for about 12 minutes.

## Ingredients

1 cup water

1/3 cup polenta or yellow cornmeal

1/2 teaspoon salt

Pinch of pepper

1 egg, well beaten

2/3 cup flour

1 teaspoon baking powder

## Hint

These can be served in soup or sprinkled with grated cheese and served as a side dish.

# SENSATIONAL TURKEY STUFFING

## Ingredients

½ cup dried apricots,
  optional
½ cup (1 stick) butter
½ pound mushrooms,
  sliced (2 cups)
1 small onion, finely
  chopped
1 cup finely chopped celery
½ cup orange or apple
  juice
2 packages (8 ounces each)
  cornbread stuffing mix
1 teaspoon salt
½ teaspoon freshly ground
  pepper
2 eggs, beaten
1 cup chopped pecans
1½ cups chicken broth

*7his* will make enough stuffing for a 14-pound turkey. If you have any extra stuffing left, place it in a baking dish. Bake it and serve with turkey gravy. Yummy!

**Makes enough stuffing for a 14-pound turkey**

Chop the apricots and soak them in boiling water for 15 minutes. Drain. Melt the butter in a saucepan and sauté the mushrooms, onion, and celery until soft.

Combine all the ingredients in a large bowl. Mix until the dressing is well moistened. If necessary, add a little more water or broth.

Stuff the dressing into the body cavities of the turkey. If you have dressing left over, place it in a buttered casserole and bake at 350°F for one hour or until golden brown. Serve with turkey gravy.

# NOODLE PUDDING (KUGEL)

*T*his is so wonderful that it can almost be served as an entrée. It goes very well with roast chicken or beef. And it will cure anyone's blahs.

**Serves 12**

Cook the noodles and drain them.

Preheat the oven to 350°F. Butter a large baking dish or a 12-cup casserole.

Melt ½ cup (1 stick) of butter. Drain the noodles and stir in the melted butter, cottage cheese, eggs, sour cream, and heavy cream. Add 1 can of apple pie filling. Toss the ingredients with a fork until well blended. Add the raisins and pour the mixture into the prepared pan.

Spread the second can of apple pie filling over the top of the noodles. Sprinkle the cornflake crumbs over the top of the noodles and cut 4 tablespoons of butter into small chunks and lay on the top of the cornflakes.

Bake for 1 hour or until the noodles are bubbly hot and golden brown. Serve hot.

## Ingredients

1 pound wide egg noodles
¾ cup (1½ sticks) butter, divided
1 pint (16 ounces) cottage cheese
6 eggs, well beaten
1 pint (16 ounces) sour cream
1 cup heavy cream or milk
2 cans (21 ounces each) apple pie filling
1 cup raisins, soaked in hot water and drained
1 cup cornflake crumbs

## Hint

For an extra-rich noodle pudding, pour a 14-ounce can of sweetened condensed milk over the top of the pudding before baking.

# RICE PILAF

## Ingredients

2 tablespoons butter

1 small onion, finely
   chopped

1½ cups long grain rice

1½ cups chicken broth

1½ cups beef broth

¼ teaspoon salt

1 teaspoon garlic powder

*T*his is great served with meat or fish. You can clean out your refrigerator and add any leftovers to the rice. I usually sauté onions and mushrooms and add water chestnuts, bok choy, chopped green and red peppers, or nuts.

**Serves 8**

Melt the butter in a saucepan and sauté the onions until they are transparent. If you choose to add mushrooms or other vegetables, sauté them now. Add the rice and the vegetables to the onions.

Add the broth to the rice mixture and bring to a boil. Cover the pot and simmer for 15 to 20 minutes or until all the liquid is absorbed.

This can be microwaved or reheated before serving.

# FRIED RICE

*This is wonderful to serve with Chinese food or on its own.*

**Serves 6**

Combine the water, salt, and rice and bring to a boil. Reduce the heat, cover, and simmer until the rice is tender and all the water is absorbed, about 20 minutes. Set the rice aside to cool.

Fry the bacon in a wok and stir until the bacon is crisp. Drain the bacon and remove all but 1 tablespoon of the drippings from the wok.

Pour half of the beaten eggs and pepper into the wok and tilt the wok so that the eggs cover the bottom of the pan. Do not scramble the egg. Cook the eggs until they are firm and then remove from the wok, roll up the egg pancake, and slice into thin strips. Cook the remaining eggs in the same manner.

Add the oil to the wok and stir-fry the ginger for 1 minute. Stir in the rice and cook and stir for 5 minutes. Add the bacon, pork, shrimp, and soy sauce and cook until thoroughly hot. Top with the chopped green onions.

## Ingredients

3 cups water

1 teaspoon salt

1½ cups uncooked long grain rice

4 slices bacon, chopped

3 eggs, well beaten

⅛ teaspoon ground pepper

2 tablespoons oil

2 teaspoons grated ginger root

8 ounces cooked pork, cut into thin slices

8 ounces cooked shrimp (salad shrimp will work)

2 tablespoons soy sauce

8 green onions, chopped

# NOODLES ROMANOFF

## Ingredients

1 package (8 ounces) wide
    noodles

3 tablespoons butter

2 tablespoons minced onion

2 tablespoons flour

1/2 teaspoon dry mustard

1 teaspoon salt

Dash of cayenne pepper

1 cup milk

1/2 teaspoon Worcestershire
    sauce

Dash of hot sauce

4 ounces sharp Cheddar
    cheese, grated (1 cup)

1 cup sour cream

1 cup cottage cheese

1/4 cup dried bread crumbs

*T*his dish is perfect with a standing rib roast (page 158). You can stir in sliced all-beef frankfurters for a great Saturday night dinner.

**Serves 6**

Cook the noodles in lightly salted boiling water according to the package directions. Add 1 tablespoon of the butter to the boiling water. Drain the noodles.

Preheat the oven to 350°F. Butter an 8-cup baking dish or casserole.

Melt the remaining 2 tablespoons butter and sauté the onion until transparent. Stir in the flour, dry mustard, salt, and cayenne pepper. Cook, stirring constantly, for 1 minute. Add the milk, all at once, and stir until the mixture thickens.

Add the Worcestershire sauce, hot sauce, and Cheddar cheese and stir until the cheese melts. Fold the sour cream and cottage cheese into the sauce and then fold in the hot cooked noodles.

Spoon into the buttered baking dish and top with bread crumbs. Bake 15 minutes.

# HOT DOGS AND BAKED BEANS

*K*ids love this. Start with the best beef hot dogs you can find. If you happen to have some cooked pork, ham, or chicken that is left over, chop it up and use it in this casserole.

**Serves 8**

Preheat the oven to 425°F. Butter a 12 × 18-inch baking pan.

In a large skillet, heat the olive oil. Sauté the green pepper and onions in the oil until the onions are transparent.

Mix in the remaining ingredients and spoon into the baking pan. Bake uncovered for 30 minutes or until the beans are bubbly.

## Ingredients

2 tablespoons olive oil or bacon drippings

1 green bell pepper, chopped

2 onions, chopped

2 cups chopped cooked pork, ham, or chicken

2 cans (15 ounces each) pork and beans

1 teaspoon garlic powder

1/2 cup molasses

3/4 cup catsup

1 teaspoon chopped garlic

2 teaspoons Italian seasoning

Few drops of hot sauce

1 pound all beef hot dogs, sliced

# VEGETABLES

$\mathcal{A}$lmost all the vegetables in the following recipes are deep-fried or creamed. So if you are looking for fat-free and heart-healthy foods, chew on a carrot.

My son Howard's idea of a green vegetable is a sour pickle. My favorite is the recipe for home-made potato chips (page 206), with fried vegetable chips (page 216) running a close second.

# THE PERFECT BAKED POTATO

*A* microwave is faster but baking a potato in a conventional oven is still better. Here are the guidelines.

Select baking potatoes—don't use new potatoes. Scrub the potatoes with a brush and prick with a fork. Rub the skin with shortening if desired.

Preheat your oven to 425°F and bake for 40 to 60 minutes. If there are other foods in the oven at the same time, bake at 350° to 375°F for 70 to 80 minutes.

When the potato is baked, roll it on a hard surface to make the inside of the potato soft. Cut a deep slit in the top of the potato and push up to plump. Top with your choice of butter or other toppings.

# COWBOY POTATOES

## Ingredients

1 package (2 pounds)
  frozen hash brown
  potatoes

1 onion, chopped

1 can (10¾ ounces) cream
  of mushroom soup

1 pint (16 ounces) sour
  cream

8 ounces (2 cups) grated
  cheese: jalapeño,
  Cheddar, or Swiss

½ cup (1 stick) butter,
  melted

1½ cups crushed cornflakes

*M*y friend, Pam Dinsmore, a nurse, made these for a physician's party. They went mad for them despite the fact that they were all on heart-healthy diets.

**Serves 8**

Preheat the oven to 350°F. Butter a 9 × 13-inch baking pan.

Break up the frozen potatoes and spread them on the bottom of the pan. Top the potatoes with the chopped onion. Mix the soup, sour cream, and cheese together and pour over the top of the onions and potatoes.

Mix the melted butter with the cornflakes and spread over the top of the potato mixture. Cover with foil and bake for 50 minutes. Remove the foil and allow the potatoes to brown for an additional 10 minutes.

# POTATO PANCAKES (LATKES)

*T*he secret of crisp and delicious potato pancakes is to use a grater instead of a food processor to grate the potatoes. I make them a few hours in advance and fry them until they are almost crisp. Then I drain them on paper towels and refry them immediately before serving them with sour cream and applesauce.

Serves 6

## Ingredients

6 medium baking potatoes
4 eggs
1 onion
1/2 cup flour or bread crumbs
1 teaspoon salt
Oil for frying
Sour cream
Applesauce

You don't have to peel the potatoes if you scrub them first. Grate the potatoes with the grater blade of the food processor or with the large holes on a hand-held grater.

Soak the grated potatoes in ice water for 15 minutes to remove the starch. Drain the potatoes using a colander and squeeze them dry.

Beat the eggs. Grate the onion and mix with the eggs, flour, and salt. Mix the drained potatoes and the egg mixture together.

Heat the oil in a deep frying pan. Drop the potato pancake mixture into the hot oil by the heaping tablespoonful and flatten the batter into a pancake, the thinner the better.

Fry on each side until golden brown and crisp. Drain on paper towels and serve at once. Serve with applesauce and/or sour cream.

# UNFRIED FRENCH FRIES

## Ingredients

6 medium potatoes, each
   cut into 8 wedges
6 tablespoons (3/4 stick)
   butter, melted, or oil
Salt and pepper
Paprika
1/2 cup freshly grated
   Parmesan cheese,
   optional

*I*t is possible to make marvelous crunchy potatoes without frying. You can substitute olive oil or vegetable oil for the butter if you prefer, and this recipe even works if you spray a cookie sheet with vegetable spray several times. You don't need to peel the potato unless you want to.

**Serves 8**

Soak the potato wedges in ice water for at least 15 minutes to remove the starch and to make the finished potato more crisp.

Drain the potatoes and remove as much water as possible by towel-drying them.

Preheat the oven to 425°F.

Spread melted butter on the bottom of the pan. Add the potato wedges, making sure that they do not touch each other. Sprinkle them with salt, pepper, and paprika. Bake for 30 minutes, turning them every 10 minutes to make sure they are brown on all sides. Sprinkle the potato wedges with the grated Parmesan cheese and bake for an additional 2 to 3 minutes. Serve hot.

# TWICE-BAKED POTATOES

These are so rich and delicious that I hardly consider them vegetables. What do you think?

**Serves 8**

Boil the unpeeled potatoes until they are tender enough to mash, about 20 minutes. Remove the potatoes from the water to cool. This can be done the day before serving.

Preheat the oven to 350°F.

Cut the potatoes in half lengthwise. Remove most of the inside of the potato, being careful not to tear the outer skin.

Put the potato insides into a large bowl and add the sour cream, melted butter, grated cheese, garlic powder, salt, and pepper. You may have to add additional cream or milk in order to mash the potato. Leave a few small lumps to impress your guests with the fact that you made these beauties.

Use a pastry tube or a spoon to put the potato filling back into the shells. Sprinkle the tops with paprika. Bake the potatoes for 30 minutes. Just before serving, place the potatoes under the broiler for a few minutes or until the tops are golden brown.

## Ingredients

4 large baking potatoes

1 cup sour cream

½ cup (1 stick) butter, melted

½ pound sharp Cheddar cheese, grated (2 cups)

1 teaspoon garlic powder or grated garlic

Salt and pepper to taste

# LUMPY MASHED POTATOES

## Ingredients

5 pounds potatoes, peeled
and cut into 2-inch cubes
1/2 cup (1 stick) butter, at
room temperature
1 1/2 cups milk
2 teaspoons salt
1 teaspoon ground pepper

Serves 8

Combine the potatoes and salt and cover with water in a heavy saucepan. Bring to a boil, cover the pot and cook until the potatoes are very tender, about 20 minutes.

Drain the water from the potatoes and mash the potatoes, leaving some lumps. Whisk in the butter, milk, salt, and pepper.

## Hint

To make garlic mashed potatoes, mix 1 to 2 tablespoons of minced garlic or garlic powder into the potatoes.

# STUFFED POTATO CRISPS

*If* you want plain vegetables, this is not the recipe for you. These crunchies are great appetizers.

**Makes 24 slices**

Preheat the oven to 425°F.

Bake the potatoes for 1 hour. If you are in a hurry you can use the microwave, but it will take almost as long.

Cool the potatoes and cut them into quarters lengthwise. Scrape away the potato pulp leaving a layer attached to the skin.

Place the skins, cut-side up, on a buttered baking dish and drizzle the skins with the melted butter. Sprinkle the skins with pepper, garlic powder, bacon, and cheese.

Bake the skins for 15 minutes or until the cheese is golden brown and puffy and the skins are crisp. Garnish with the chives.

## Ingredients

6 large potatoes, scrubbed clean

1/2 cup (1 stick) butter, melted

Freshly ground pepper

Garlic powder

8 strips bacon, fried crisp and crumbled

2 cups grated Cheddar cheese

2 tablespoons chopped chives for garnish

# POTATO CHIPS

## Ingredients

4 large baking potatoes
Vegetable oil for deep-
    frying
Salt and granulated garlic
    to taste

*T*his recipe for homemade potato chips is supreme. There are special machines for slicing the chips, but you can use the slicer on your food processor or your potato peeler if you're adept. No need to peel the potatoes first.

Serves 8

## Hint

The chips can be fried several hours before serving, then refried for a minute or two right before they are eaten. This will result in an even crisper chip.

Slice the potatoes and soak the chips in ice water for at least 15 minutes. Use a colander to drain the water and dry the chips on a terry towel, removing as much moisture as possible.

Heat the oil in a deep fryer to 375°F. Fry the chips, about 1 cup at a time, for 1 to 2 minutes, turning the chips until both sides are golden brown and crisp. Remove with a slotted spoon and drain on paper towels. Season with salt and garlic to taste. Serve hot.

# SWEET POTATO CASSEROLE

If Thanksgiving is your idea of the perfect comfort dinner, you'll love this casserole. It doesn't have to be a holiday to enjoy this.

**Serves 8**

Preheat the oven to 375°F. Butter an 8-cup baking dish and set it aside. Bake the potatoes for 40 minutes or until tender.

Lower the oven temperature to 350°F.

Peel and mash the baked sweet potatoes and add butter, cream, and wine. Add the cinnamon, salt, nutmeg, orange peel, and pepper to taste.

Spoon the sweet potato mixture into the prepared baking dish. Dot with butter and sprinkle with chopped pecans.

Bake for 30 minutes.

## Ingredients

6 large sweet potatoes

4 tablespoons (½ stick) butter, softened

½ cup light cream

½ cup red wine

½ teaspoon cinnamon

½ teaspoon salt

½ teaspoon nutmeg

1 tablespoon freshly grated orange peel

Pepper

Butter as needed

Chopped pecans or walnuts, optional

# STIR-FRY VEGETABLES

## Ingredients

2 tablespoons peanut oil

1 small slice ginger root

1 bunch broccoli, cut into florets

1 small head cauliflower, cut into florets

½ pound mushrooms, sliced (2 cups)

½ cup sliced green bell pepper

½ cup sliced red bell pepper

2 cups sliced bok choy or celery, cut on the diagonal

2 cloves garlic, minced

1 teaspoon pepper

1 teaspoon salt

2 tablespoons soy sauce

4 ounces sharp Cheddar cheese, grated (1 cup)

In every life a few vegetables must appear and these are delicious. Don't forget the Cheddar cheese!

**Serves 6 to 8**

Heat the oil in a wok or large frying pan and rub the ginger on the sides of the pan. Discard the used ginger.

Place the broccoli and cauliflower florets on the bottom of the wok. Layer the mushrooms, green and red peppers, and bok choy on the top. Add the garlic, salt, and pepper. Cover and cook over medium heat for 10 minutes or until the vegetables are crisp. Stir the vegetables until well mixed.

Add the soy sauce and grated cheese and serve hot.

# CHEESE- AND BACON- STUFFED TOMATOES

It should be obvious by now that even the vegetable recipes in this book are designed for comfort, not health. Even my vegetarian friend, Shira Frank, eats almost nothing green!

**Serves 4**

Preheat the oven to 400°F. Butter a 9 × 12-inch baking dish.

Remove the tops of the tomatoes and carefully scoop out the pulp of the tomato and set it aside. Drain the tomatoes upside down on a rack.

Cook the bacon until it is almost done. Drain off the fat and add the green pepper and onion and sauté until the onion is transparent. Remove the skillet from the heat and stir in the cheese and tomato pulp. Fill the hollowed tomato shells with this mixture and sprinkle the crumbs on the top. Dot with butter.

Bake for 30 minutes.

## Ingredients

4 medium tomatoes, very firm

12 slices bacon, cut into pieces

$\frac{1}{2}$ cup chopped green bell pepper

$\frac{1}{2}$ cup finely chopped onion

6 ounces Cheddar cheese, grated ($1\frac{1}{2}$ cups)

2 tablespoons cracker crumbs or dry bread crumbs

1 tablespoon butter

# TEMPURA MUSHROOMS

## Ingredients

¼ cup flour

Pinch of salt

1 egg

⅓ cup flat beer

Oil for deep-frying

1 pound small mushrooms,
    washed and dried

1½ cups dry bread crumbs

*T*hese are memorable appetizers. The recipe works well with other vegetables including onion rings, thinly sliced carrots, cauliflower florets, green beans, parsley sprigs, sweet potato slices, or chunks of eggplant or green and red bell peppers.

**Serves 6**

Mix the flour and salt together in a small bowl. Beat the egg and beer together until smooth, and add to the flour mixture. Let the batter stand at room temperature for 1 hour.

Heat the oil in a deep fryer to 375°F. Dip the dried vegetables into the batter and then roll them in the bread crumbs.

Fry a few at a time in the hot oil until golden brown on all sides. Serve hot with a tangy dipping sauce of mayonnaise with a little catsup and horseradish mixed into it.

# FRENCH-FRIED ONION RINGS

---

*I*t's no wonder that my grandchildren love my vegetables. They are fried, crunchy, and a great source of comfort, calories, and flavor.

**Serves 6**

Combine the egg, milk, and vegetable oil and mix well. Stir in the flour, baking powder, and salt and mix until smooth.

In a deep frying pan or a deep fryer, heat oil to 350°F. Towel-dry the onion rings, removing as much water as possible. Toss the onion slices and batter together. Try to separate the onion rings and, using long-handled tongs, dip the onion rings into the hot oil.

Turn the rings to make sure they are fried on both sides and drain on paper towels. Serve hot.

## Ingredients

1 egg
1 cup milk
1 tablespoon vegetable oil
1 cup flour
1 teaspoon baking powder
Pinch of salt
Oil for frying
3 large onions, sliced and soaked in ice water for 1 hour

# GREEN BEAN BAKE

## Ingredients

1 can (10¾ ounces) cream
of mushroom soup

¼ cup milk

3 cans (16 ounces each)
whole or sliced green
beans, drained

1 can (8 ounces) sliced
water chestnuts

1 can (6 ounces) French-
fried onion rings

*T*his combination of is one of my favorites.

**Serves 6**

Preheat oven to 350°F. Mix together all the ingredients and place in an 8-cup casserole dish. Bake for 30 minutes. Serve hot.

# FRENCH-FRIED CAULIFLOWER

$7$his recipe is fabulous. The cauliflower is crisp on the outside, creamy on the inside.

**Serves 6 to 8**

Wash the cauliflower and separate into florets. Cook in boiling water until barely tender, about 10 minutes. Drain and cool thoroughly.

Combine the eggs, water, salt, and pepper and blend well.

Roll the cooked cauliflower in flour or place the cauliflower in a plastic bag with the flour and shake to coat. Dip the floured cauliflower into the egg batter and place on a rack to drain.

Roll the dipped cauliflower in bread crumbs.

Heat the oil in a deep fryer to 375°F. Fry the cauliflower for 1 minute or until golden brown. Drain on paper towels and serve hot.

## Ingredients

1 head cauliflower
2 eggs, well beaten
1/4 cup water
1/4 teaspoon salt
Pinch of pepper
1/2 cup flour
1 cup dry bread crumbs
Oil for deep-frying

## Hint

This is also great using sliced tomatoes or cooked carrots.

# CREAMED SPINACH

## Ingredients

1 small onion, minced
2 cloves garlic, crushed
2 tablespoons butter
1 tablespoon flour
1 package (10 ounces)
   frozen spinach, cooked
   and drained
1/4 teaspoon salt
1 cup sour cream
3 slices of bacon, cooked
   crisp and crumbled,
   optional

## Hint

You can substitute buttermilk
or heavy whipping cream for
the sour cream.

*O*ld cartoons show Popeye gaining strength from gulping a can of cooked spinach. The rest of us prefer it creamed.

**Serves 4**

Sauté the onion and the garlic in the butter until the onion is transparent. Stir in the flour and cook for 1 minute. Add the cooked spinach and salt and cook, stirring constantly over low heat, until the mixture is thick.

Remove from heat and add the sour cream and blend. Fold in the crumbled bacon. Serve hot.

# EGGPLANT PARMIGIANA

*I*t's hard to tell that this is a vegetable because it is totally acceptable to children and adults alike.

**Serves 4**

Preheat the oven to 325°F.

Combine the eggs with the oregano, basil, salt, pepper, and garlic powder. Dip the eggplant slices into the egg mixture and then into the bread crumbs.

Heat enough olive oil in a large frying pan to keep the eggplant from sticking. Brown the slices quickly in the hot oil.

Arrange the browned eggplant slices in a baking dish and cover with half the tomato sauce, mushrooms, mozzarella cheese, and Parmesan.

Repeat with the other half of the eggplant.

Bake for 45 minutes or until heated through and bubbly. Serve hot with garlic bread.

## Ingredients

2 eggs, beaten

1/2 teaspoon oregano

1/4 teaspoon dried basil

Salt and pepper to taste

1/2 teaspoon garlic powder

1 large eggplant, sliced 1/4 inch thick

1 cup fine dry bread crumbs

Olive oil for browning

2 cups tomato sauce

1/2 pound fresh mushrooms, sliced (2 cups)

1 pound thinly sliced mozzarella cheese

1 cup grated Parmesan cheese

# VEGETABLE CHIPS

## Ingredients

1 large sweet potato
1 large baking potato
2 carrots
1 large beet
1 large taro root
1 large turnip
Vegetable oil for frying

*T*hese are relatively new on the gourmet market and they are fantastic—even better than potato chips. You can use any vegetable you feel is suitable for deep-frying.

**Serves 4 to 6**

Slice the vegetables using a food processor or the slicing side of a grater. Keep the slices as thin and broad as possible by cutting them on an angle.

Soak the vegetables for 15 minutes in ice water to remove the starch. Towel-dry the vegetables.

Heat the oil to 375°F in a deep fryer. Drop a few vegetable slices at a time into the fryer to allow them to brown completely. Remove the cooked vegetables chips from the fryer with a slotted spoon and drain them on paper towels.

Salt and serve hot or cold.

Store in a tightly sealed container to retain freshness.

# CREAMED CORN

Creamed corn tied with creamed spinach as the top comfort food vegetable.

Serves 6

## Ingredients

1 slice white bread

¼ cup water

1 can (16 ounces) creamed corn

1 tablespoon flour

2 tablespoons (¼ stick) butter, melted

½ cup milk or light cream

3 egg yolks, well beaten

3 egg whites

¼ teaspoon salt

Preheat the oven to 350°F. Butter a 6-cup casserole.

Soak the bread in the water and then squeeze dry and mash with a fork. Add the creamed corn, flour, melted butter, milk, and egg yolks and stir until well blended.

Whip the egg whites with the salt until stiff and fold into the corn mixture. Pour into the buttered casserole and bake for 30 to 40 minutes or until a knife inserted in the center of the casserole comes out clean and dry.

# SAUCES, DRESSINGS, AND CONDIMENTS

*T*he sauces and dressings in this chapter will add a special touch to your favorite foods—without a lot of fuss.

Mustard, for instance, is very simple to make. If you use your imagination and some unique ingredients you can create your own signature mustard that will please you, your family, and guests. Jars of homemade mustard make wonderful hostess gifts.

Salsa is wonderful on everything from a salad to a baked potato. Making it yourself ensures freshness and great taste. Try the chutney or mayonaisse—you may discover a new favorite.

# BASIC UNCOOKED MUSTARD

## Ingredients

½ cup dry mustard
1 tablespoon sour cream
½ cup water (or less)
Salt, pepper, and any seasonings you prefer

*M*any of the gourmet mustards on the market today are variations on this theme. Be courageous—experiment with different vinegars and spices.

**Makes 1 cup**

Mix the dry mustard, sour cream, and enough water to make a spreadable paste. Season to taste. Keep refrigerated between uses.

# DELI MUSTARD

## Ingredients

5 tablespoons dry mustard

¼ cup mustard seeds

¼ cup warm water

1 cup cider vinegar

1 large clove garlic, crushed

2 tablespoons firmly packed
   dark brown sugar

1 teaspoon salt

¼ teaspoon ground ginger

¼ teaspoon allspice

¼ teaspoon cinnamon

1 to 2 teaspoons honey,
   optional

*A* must for your great sandwiches. This is dark brown, spicy, and slightly sweet. Another good hostess gift.

**Makes 2 cups**

Blend together the dry mustard, mustard seeds, and warm water in a heavy saucepan. Set aside.

In another saucepan, combine the remaining ingredients except the honey. Bring to a boil, reduce the heat, and simmer gently for 5 minutes. Cool for a few minutes and whisk the vinegar mixture into the mustard mixture.

Continue to simmer the mustard for about 10 minutes or until it bubbles gently around the edges. Scrape the mixture into a bowl and let it stand for 2 hours.

Use a food processor to blend the mixture thoroughly. Add honey to taste. Place the mustard in a jar and refrigerate. This will keep for several months.

# BASIC COOKED MUSTARD

**Makes 1 cup**

Blend all the ingredients except for the egg yolks and let stand for several hours. Beat the egg yolks into the mustard mixture and cook in the top of a double boiler over hot, but not boiling, water stirring constantly until the mixture is slightly thickened—about 5 minutes.

Cover and store in the refrigerator for up to 3 months.

## Ingredients

¼ cup dry mustard
¼ cup white wine vinegar
⅓ cup dry white wine
1 tablespoon sugar
½ teaspoon salt
3 egg yolks

## Hint

To make spicy mustard, follow the basic recipe. Add ¼ teaspoon turmeric and ¼ teaspoon cloves at the same time that you add the egg yolks.

# DIJON MUSTARD

## Ingredients

2 cups dry white wine
1 cup chopped onion
3 cloves garlic, minced
1/2 cup dry mustard
2 tablespoons honey
1 tablespoon vegetable oil
1 teaspoon salt
Few drops of Tabasco sauce

**Makes 3 cups**

Combine the wine, onion, and garlic in a saucepan and heat to boiling. Lower the heat and simmer for 5 minutes.

Pour the mixture into a bowl and cool. Strain the wine mixture into the dry mustard and beat until very smooth. Add the honey, oil, salt, and Tabasco and heat slowly, stirring constantly until the mixture thickens. Cool, pour into a glass jar with a tight fitting lid, and store in the refrigerator.

Allow the flavor to ripen for at least 2 days before serving.

# MUSTARD SAUCE

*Ingredients*

This sauce is especially good with the perfect steak (page 160).

**Makes 1 cup**

½ cup sugar
1½ teaspoons cornstarch
1 tablespoon dry mustard
¼ teaspoon salt
1 egg yolk
½ cup hot cream
2½ teaspoons cider vinegar

Mix together the sugar, cornstarch, dry mustard, and salt in a heavy saucepan.

Beat the egg yolk slightly and add to the dry ingredients. Stir until smooth. Slowly add the hot cream and mix thoroughly.

Cook over medium heat, stirring constantly, until the sauce thickens.

Slowly add the vinegar and mix well. Remove from the heat and pour into a jar with a tight fitting lid. Store in the refrigerator.

# HOT PEPPER JELLY

## Ingredients

1½ cups cider vinegar

5 cups sugar

1½ cups chopped red bell
pepper

1½ teaspoons dried,
crushed red pepper
flakes

1 jar (6 ounces) liquid
pectin

Few drops of red food
coloring

$\mathcal{P}$our this over an 8-ounce package of cream cheese and serve with crackers or crudités. It's a great appetizer.

**Makes 6 cups**

Combine the vinegar and sugar in a saucepan and bring to a boil. Add both kinds of pepper and boil again, stirring constantly. Remove the mixture from the heat and stir in the fruit pectin and food coloring. Pour into sterilized jars and seal with hot wax.

# CRANBERRY CHUTNEY

If you are a curry fan, you know that chutney is expensive to buy. This is simple to make and makes a great hostess gift.

**Makes 4 cups**

Peel the oranges, remove the fiber and membrane, and cut into chunks. Save enough of the orange peel to make 1/4 cup fine orange slivers.

Combine the orange peel slivers, juice, cranberries, sugar, ginger, Tabasco, cinnamon, garlic, curry, and raisins in a saucepan.

Cook and stir the mixture until the sugar dissolves and the cranberries pop open. Remove the mixture from the heat and discard the garlic and the cinnamon stick. Add the oranges and mix lightly. Serve hot or cold.

Chutney can be stored in a tightly sealed jar in the refrigerator for months or it can be poured into sterilized jars and sealed with wax.

## Ingredients

4 oranges

1/3 cup orange juice

1 pound fresh cranberries

2 cups sugar

1/4 cup diced crystallized ginger

1/2 teaspoon Tabasco sauce

1 whole cinnamon stick

1 clove garlic, peeled

3/4 teaspoon curry powder

3/4 cup raisins

# CLARIFIED BUTTER

*T*he purpose of clarifying butter is to remove the excess liquid it contains. You can heat clarified butter to a high temperature without having it smoke.

Melt butter in a saucepan over low heat or in a microwave and allow the melted butter to stand for several minutes.

Skim and discard any foam that rises to the surface and then pour the clear, oily butter into a container and refrigerate it. The butter should keep for up to 3 months.

If there is a milky residue at the bottom of the pan, discard it.

You can use a double boiler for this process if you prefer.

# RED CHILI SAUCE (ENCHILADA SAUCE)

*G*etting this recipe was incredibly difficult. Everyone has a different version of how to make this sauce. The key ingredient is lard, but you can use bacon drippings.

This is wonderful on everything from enchiladas to scrambled eggs. It will make you famous!

**Makes 3 cups**

Heat the lard in a saucepan and stir in the flour. Cook, stirring constantly, until the mixture is slightly brown.

Add the chili powder and bouillon and mix well. Cook until the sauce is smooth. Add the salt, garlic, oregano, and cumin.

Add more chili powder if you prefer a hotter flavor. Simmer for 30 minutes, stirring occasionally.

Store the sauce in the refrigerator for up to a month or freeze it.

## Ingredients

2 tablespoons lard or bacon drippings

2 tablespoons flour

1/4 to 3/4 cup mild red chili powder

2 cups beef bouillon or water

1 teaspoon salt

1 clove garlic (or more), minced

Pinch of oregano

Pinch of cumin

# MILD SALSA

## Ingredients

½ cup finely diced fresh
tomato
½ cup finely diced Spanish
onion
½ cup finely diced fresh
green chiles (the mild
kind), stems, seeds, and
skins removed before
chopping
1 clove garlic, minced
½ teaspoon salt

**Makes 1½ cups**

Combine all the ingredients and refrigerate
until served.

# SALSA FRESCA

This recipe has many more ingredients than the mild salsa, but it is special enough to give as a hostess gift.

**Makes 3½ cups**

Combine all the ingredients and mix well. Refrigerate overnight to allow the flavors to develop.

## Ingredients

1 can (16 ounces) chopped tomatoes, drained

1 fresh tomato, finely chopped

2 tablespoons red wine vinegar

2 tablespoons minced Spanish onion

2 tablespoons fresh lime juice

2 tablespoons minced parsley

1 heaping teaspoon coarse salt

1 clove garlic, minced

¼ cup water

2 tablespoons minced fresh chives

1 teaspoon finely minced serrano chile

¼ cup diced canned green chiles

6 tablespoons minced green bell pepper

Pinch of oregano

Pinch of cumin

# GARDEN SALSA

## Ingredients

1 cup fresh cilantro
2 cloves garlic
1 jalapeño pepper
1 bunch small radishes
½ cup diced red onion
1 small green bell pepper,
   cored
1 large tomato
2 tablespoons olive oil
2 teaspoons lemon juice
½ teaspoon salt

*T*his is a wonderful salsa, full of unusual vegetables, and it tastes marvelous on everything, including a plain baked potato.

**Makes 2 cups**

Place all the ingredients in a food processor and chop. Refrigerate for at least 1 hour to allow the flavors to blend.

Serve with chips as a dip or with meat, fish, or chicken.

# MOMMA'S MAYONNAISE

## Ingredients

2 egg yolks
2 tablespoons vinegar
1 teaspoon mustard
Pinch of salt
1/4 cup sugar
1 cup vegetable oil

*I*f you are a person who believes a sandwich needs fine mayonnaise and who loves potato salad laced with mayonnaise, you'll find comfort in this recipe. This will keep well in your refrigerator for several weeks.

**Makes 1 1/2 cups**

In a blender or a food processor, mix together all the ingredients except for the oil. When everything is well mixed, add the oil very slowly while the processor is running. Blend until thick.

You can add garlic, cayenne pepper or any seasoning your heart desires to make your mayonnaise unique and flavorful.

# SWEETENED CONDENSED MILK

## Ingredients

4 cups instant powdered
 milk (skim milk works)
1 cup hot water
2 cups sugar
4 tablespoons (½ stick)
 butter, melted

**S**weetened condensed milk is expensive and I am usually out of it just when I need it to make something marvelous. Now you can make it yourself and always have a supply on hand.

**Makes 3 cups**

Mix the ingredients in a blender or food processor and store in the refrigerator. This gets better after a few days—thicker and richer.

# WHITE SAUCE MIX

$\mathcal{Y}$ ou can use this as a basis for creamed foods as well as macaroni and cheese.

**Makes 2 cups of sauce when mixed with 2 cups of water**

Blend the ingredients using a food processor until the mixture is the thickness and texture of coarse salt. Refrigerate in a tightly sealed container until ready for use. This will keep for several months.

To make one cup of white sauce, use $1/2$ cup of mix and 1 cup of water.

Heat until thick, stirring constantly, and add cheese and flavorings to taste.

*Ingredients*

$2^{2}/_{3}$ cups powdered milk
1 cup (2 sticks) butter
$1^{1}/_{2}$ cups flour
1 tablespoon salt

# RUSSIAN DRESSING

## Ingredients

¹/₂ bottle (12-ounce size)
    chili sauce
¹/₂ cup mayonnaise
1 teaspoon prepared
    horseradish
Juice of ¹/₂ lemon

*U*se this on Reuben or turkey sandwiches.

**Makes 1 cup**

Whisk all ingredients together until smooth.

# PESTO SAUCE

## Ingredients

8 cloves garlic
1 cup olive oil
2 cups chopped fresh basil
1 cup parsley
2 teaspoons salt
Pepper

*T*his is a hot item on the menus of upscale restaurants. It's a thick, green sauce that can be used as a dressing for hard boiled eggs, or raw or cooked vegetables. It's also delicious with seafood and pasta.

If you grow your own basil, you can make lots of this and keep it frozen.

**Makes 2 cups**

In a blender, place the garlic and 1/4 cup of the olive oil together with some of the greens. Purée, adding oil a little at a time and then adding more greens.

Continue this until all the greens have been processed into a thick, green sauce. You may have to add additional olive oil so that the finished mixture is the consistency of mayonnaise.

Season with salt and pepper and put into a jar with a tight fitting lid. Pesto will keep in your refrigerator for several months.

# BLUE CHEESE DRESSING

## Ingredients

1/2 pound blue cheese

6 tablespoons heavy cream

1 tablespoon lemon juice

3 tablespoons mayonnaise

2 tablespoons olive oil

2 cloves garlic, mashed

1/2 teaspoon Worcestershire
   sauce

Few drops of hot sauce

Salt and pepper to taste

*7*his is wonderful dressing to use for salads, crudités, or deep-fried vegetables. It's also great on a baked potato.

**Makes 2 cups**

Use a food processor to combine the blue cheese, cream, and lemon juice. Process until smooth and let stand for 5 minutes.

Add the mayonnaise and gradually beat in the olive oil and garlic, and season to taste with Worcestershire sauce, hot sauce, salt, and pepper.

## Hint

If you want the blue cheese to remain in lumps, mash the ingredients together with a fork instead of the food processor.

# SPAGHETTI SAUCE SUPREME

This is a sauce that you cook for hours. You can use a Crock-Pot if you prefer because the longer this cooks, the thicker and richer it will be.

**Makes 6 cups**

## Ingredients

1 pound lean ground beef

4 cloves garlic, minced

2 tablespoons olive oil

2 large carrots, chopped

3 medium onions, chopped

10 cups tomato juice

6 tablespoons tomato paste

2 cans (1 pound each)
   Italian plum tomatoes

4 tablespoons chopped
   fresh parsley

1 1/2 teaspoons oregano

1/2 teaspoons dried basil

3 bay leaves

2 tablespoons butter

1 teaspoon chili powder

Sauté the beef and garlic in the olive oil until the meat is brown. Place in a large pot.

Sauté the carrots and onions in the same frying pan you used for the beef. If necessary, add a little olive oil.

Cook over very low heat for 10 minutes. Add the vegetables to the pot. Add all the remaining ingredients and cook over very low heat for 2 or more hours, stirring occasionally.

# STEAK MARINADE

## Ingredients

1 can (10¾ ounces) beef
  broth
⅓ cup soy sauce
1 teaspoon seasoned salt
¼ cup grated onion
3 cloves garlic, minced
1 tablespoon lemon juice
2 tablespoons brown sugar

*T*his marinade is for meat and potato lovers. It will tenderize the meat and add great flavor. Be sure to marinate the meat for at least 24 hours.

**Makes 1½ cups**

Combine all the ingredients and pour over the steak. Refrigerate for up to 24 hours. Discard marinade before cooking the meat.

# DESSERTS

My grandson was four years old and it was breakfast time. He said he wanted German chocolate cake for breakfast but I argued that it was being saved for after dinner. He said, "Lets eat dinner first." Of course, he was right. Let's eat dessert first.

# FLORENTINES

*T*his recipe is relatively simple and the result is a sweet and crunchy cookie. These dainties can be served with melted chocolate spread on one side or sandwiched together, or rolled and filled with whipped cream.

**Makes about 6 dozen cookies**

Preheat the oven to 375°F. Butter 2 cookie sheets and dust them lightly with flour. I use a large plastic shaker filled with flour to make this job easy.

Combine the flour, baking powder, salt, and sugar in a mixer bowl. Beat in the milk, vanilla, corn syrup, and melted butter until well blended. Blend in the oats and chopped nuts. Drop the batter by the teaspoonful onto the prepared cookie sheets and bake for 8 to 10 minutes or until the edges of the cookies become brown.

While the cookies are baking, lightly dust a few paper towels with powdered sugar. This will prevent the cookies from sticking to the paper. Very carefully remove the hot cookies from the baking pan and let them cool on the paper towels.

If you are going to roll the cookies you must do so while the cookies are very hot or they become brittle. Roll these delicacies around a 1-inch dowel when they are warm. Fill the cooled cookies with whipped cream.

## Ingredients

¼ cup flour
½ teaspoon baking powder
½ teaspoon salt
1 cup sugar
¼ cup milk
1 teaspoon vanilla
¼ cup corn syrup
½ cup (1 stick) butter, melted
1 cup rolled oats
1 cup chopped nuts (walnuts or pecans)
Whipped cream, optional

# PEANUT BUTTER BARS

## Ingredients

1 cup sugar

1 cup firmly packed brown sugar

1 1/2 cups light corn syrup

1 cup crunchy peanut butter

2 cups cornflakes

1 cup peanuts, roasted and salted

## Topping

1 package (12 ounces) semisweet chocolate chips

2 tablespoons (1/4 stick) butter

4 tablespoons creamy peanut butter

*T*his is for those of you who love peanut butter. This is as good as a candy bar and no baking is required, so the kids can help.

**Makes 2 dozen bars**

Grease a 9 × 13-inch baking pan.

Cook the sugars and syrup together over low heat, stirring constantly. Boil for 1 minute. Stir in the peanut butter and stir until melted. Fold in the cornflakes and peanuts and pour into the prepared pan. Smooth to fill the pan evenly.

Melt all the topping ingredients together over low heat and pour over the bar mixture. Cool and cut into 1 × 2-inch bars.

## Hint

If you microwave the corn syrup bottle for 1 minute on high, you will find the corn syrup pours and measures more easily.

# MACAROONS

I think this is a great recipe for macaroons. But then, I consider macaroons a comfort food.

**Makes 3 dozen cookies**

## Ingredients

2½ cups flaked coconut

1 cup sugar

⅓ cup flour

¼ teaspoon salt

4 egg whites

1 teaspoon almond extract or flavoring

1 cup finely chopped almonds, optional

Preheat the oven to 325°F.

Mix together the coconut, sugar, flour, and salt. Use an electric mixer to whip the egg whites until they form soft peaks. Fold the egg whites into the coconut mixture. Stir in the almond extract. If you want crunchy macaroons, add the chopped almonds.

Use a pastry tube with a star tip to shape tiny macaroons on an ungreased cookie sheet covered with parchment paper, or drop the mixture by the teaspoonful onto the cookie sheet.

Bake for 20 minutes or until the edges of the macaroons are golden brown. Cool and serve.

## Hint

Melt 1 cup of chocolate chips per batch of macaroons. Stab the macaroons with a fork and dip the bottoms in melted chocolate. Place the cookies on waxed paper until the chocolate is set. Drizzle the remaining melted chocolate over the tops of the cookies.

## Ingredients

2½ cups flour

½ teaspoon baking soda

Pinch of salt

1 cup firmly packed dark
    brown sugar

½ cup sugar

1 cup (2 sticks) butter, at
    room temperature

1 tablespoon vanilla

2 large eggs

1 package (12 ounces)
    chocolate chips

1 cup chopped pecans or
    walnuts, optional

# CHOCOLATE CHIP COOKIES

*T*his is my favorite chocolate chip cookie recipe. Almost everyone agrees that, hot or cold, soft or crispy, chocolate chip cookies are what they reach for when they need comforting.

**Makes 50 small cookies**

Preheat the oven to 325°F. You will need at least 2 ungreased cookie sheets. Cover them with parchment paper if desired.

Combine the flour, baking soda, and salt and set aside. Blend the sugars in a mixer and cream with the softened butter. Scrape down the sides and bottom of the bowl. Add the vanilla and eggs; mix until light and fluffy. Add the flour mixture. Do not overmix. Add the chocolate chips and nuts.

Drop the dough by teaspoonfuls onto the prepared cookie sheet 2 inches apart—these cookies spread. Bake 20 minutes or until golden brown. Transfer the cookies to a cold surface using a spatula.

# OATMEAL RAISIN COOKIES

*7hese* cookies are soft and chewy and so delicious that they are almost at the top of my list of comfort foods. The secret is to soak the raisins in very hot water for at least 15 minutes and drain them before adding them to the batter. You can add brandy or rum to the water if you like.

**Makes 4 dozen cookies**

Preheat the oven to 350°F. Line 2 cookie sheets with parchment paper. Don't grease the cookie sheets.

Using a mixer, cream the sugars and butter until light and fluffy. Add the flour, baking soda, salt, and cinnamon and mix well.

Add the beaten eggs, drained raisins, and vanilla together with the oatmeal and nuts. The dough will be soft. Drop by heaping teaspoonfuls onto the prepared cookie sheet 2 inches apart. These cookies will spread.

Bake for 15 minutes or until slightly browned. Remove the cookies from the oven and cool them on paper towels. Sprinkle the cookies with cinnamon-sugar mixture while they are warm.

## Ingredients

1 cup firmly packed dark brown sugar
1/2 cup sugar
1 cup (2 sticks) butter, at room temperature
2 1/2 cups flour
2 teaspoons baking soda
1 teaspoon salt
1 teaspoon cinnamon
3 large eggs, well beaten
1 cup raisins, soaked in hot water and drained
1 tablespoon vanilla
2 cups oatmeal
1 cup chopped nuts
1 tablespoon cinnamon mixed with 1/4 cup sugar

## Hint

I keep a mixture of cinnamon and sugar in a sugar shaker so it's ready for topping cookies and toast.

# BISCOTTI

## Ingredients

2 eggs

1 cup sugar

1 cup vegetable or
   canola oil

2½ cups flour

1 teaspoon baking soda

1 teaspoon baking powder

1 tablespoon vanilla

1 cup chopped nuts
   (almonds, walnuts,
   pecans, or hazelnuts)

1 cup chocolate chips,
   optional

½ cup raisins, optional

1 tablespoon of cinnamon
   mixed with ¼ cup sugar

*T*his is a very old recipe. It is also remarkably simple considering that biscotti is very expensive to buy. These twice-baked cookies, also known as *Mandelbröt*, stay fresh forever—they actually get better when they are stale. These are less dry than commercial biscotti because the cookies will be fresh when you bake them. I always bake a double batch to keep in my pantry.

**Makes 3 dozen biscotti**

Preheat the oven to 300°F. Cover a cookie sheet with parchment paper or spray it lightly with nonstick cooking spray.

Mix the eggs and sugar until very thick and lemon colored. Add the oil slowly. Slowly add the flour, baking soda, and baking powder. Add the vanilla, nuts, and chocolate chips and raisins if desired. Chill the dough for several hours or overnight.

This is a soft and sticky dough. When you are ready to bake the biscotti, shape the dough into 2 to 4 small loaves using your dampened fingers. Since this dough spreads, don't place the loaves close together on the prepared cookie sheets. Use 2 cookie sheets if necessary. Bake the biscotti until it is golden brown, about 30 minutes. Remove the cookie sheets from the oven and sprinkle the biscotti with the cinnamon and sugar.

Cool the biscotti slightly. Use a sharp hand spatula or a knife to cut into diagonal slices. Separate the slices on the cookie sheet.

Return cookie sheets to the oven. Turn off the oven heat and leave trays in the oven overnight so the cookies can become dry—or twice-baked as they are known.

*For chocolate biscotti:* Add ¼ cup sifted cocoa in with the flour in the basic biscotti recipe, then proceed with instructions.

*For reduced-calorie biscotti:* Replace ½ cup of the oil in the basic biscotti recipe with ½ cup unsweetened applesauce. Omit the nuts and chocolate. Proceed with instructions.

# HEALTHFUL SOFT AND CHEWY COOKIES

## Ingredients

1 cup (2 sticks) butter, at
    room temperature

1 cup sugar

1 cup firmly packed brown
    sugar

1 large egg

1 cup oil

1 tablespoon vanilla

1 cup cornflake crumbs

1 cup instant oats

1/2 cup shredded coconut

1/2 cup chopped walnuts,
    pecans, or nuts of your
    choice

3 1/2 cups flour

1 teaspoon salt, optional

1 teaspoon baking soda

## Hint

For another version, you can add 3 large candy bars (Snickers, Milky Way, or Baby Ruth) cut into chunks. These always bring rave reviews from cookie fans. Don't even think about adding candy bars to these cookies for a diabetic!

These cookies are soft, chewy, and moist. You can substitute fructose for the granulated sugar if you are serving these to a diabetic. Use 2/3 cup fructose in place of one cup of the white sugar. If you replace the brown sugar, the cookie will have a different flavor but it is still delicious.

**Makes 100 cookies**

Preheat the oven to 350°F. Spray 2 cookie sheets lightly with vegetable oil or place a sheet of parchment paper on each ungreased cookie sheet.

Using a mixer, cream together the butter and sugars until light and fluffy. Add the egg and oil, mixing well after each addition. Mix in the vanilla, then add the cornflake crumbs, oats, coconut, and nuts. Add the flour, salt, and baking soda.

Chill the batter for 1 hour. Form into balls the size of a walnut. Place the cookie balls on the prepared cookie sheets and flatten them with moistened fingertips.

Bake for 12 minutes or until they are golden brown. Remove the cookie sheet from the oven and let the cookies cool for a few minutes before removing them from the tray and placing them on paper toweling to complete the cooling. Store in an airtight container.

# WHITE CHOCOLATE BROWNIES (BLONDIES)

*W*hite chocolate lovers—this one is for you. White chocolate brownies must not be over-baked or they become very dry.

**Makes 18 bars**

Preheat the oven to 350°F and spray a 9-inch square baking pan with cooking spray and dust it lightly with flour.

In the top of a double boiler, combine 5 tablespoons of the butter and 6 ounces of the chocolate and melt them together. Stir until smooth.

Remove the chocolate mixture from the heat and blend in the sugar and vanilla. Stir in the flour and baking powder. Beat the egg whites until stiff, then fold into the chocolate mixture. Add the chopped pecans. Spread the batter into the prepared pan and bake for 25 minutes or until the brownies are a light golden brown. *Do not overbake.*

Melt the remaining 5 tablespoons butter and 6 ounces chocolate in the top of a double boiler and spread the melted chocolate over the cooled brownies. When the chocolate is set, cut the brownies into bars.

## Ingredients

10 tablespoons (1 1/4 stick) butter, at room temperature
12 ounces white chocolate or white chocolate coating wafers
1 cup sugar
1 teaspoon vanilla
4 egg whites
1 1/4 cups flour
1/2 teaspoon baking powder
1/2 cup chopped pecans

# CARAMEL BROWNIES

## Ingredients

1 pound caramels,
  unwrapped

$2/3$ cup evaporated milk

1 box Swiss chocolate cake
  mix

$3/4$ cup ($1 1/2$ sticks) butter,
  melted

1 cup chopped nuts of your
  choice

1 package (12 ounces)
  semisweet chocolate
  chips

## Hint

Eliminate the caramels
and evaporated milk and
use half a container of
apple-dipping caramel
sauce, available in the produce department of large
supermarkets.

*T*hese are totally decadent and delicious—
worth the effort of unwrapping all the caramels.

**Makes 6 dozen (1-inch) squares**

Preheat the oven to 350°F. Grease and flour a
9 × 13-inch baking pan.

Melt the caramels together with $1/3$ cup of
evaporated milk in the top of a double boiler. Set
aside to cool.

Combine the cake mix with the remaining $1/3$
cup of evaporated milk, butter, and nuts. The
dough will be stiff. Press half of the dough into
the prepared pan. Bake 6 minutes.

Spread the chocolate chips over the dough
and top with the caramel mixture. Sprinkle the
remaining dough over the top. Bake the brownies an additional 15 to 18 minutes, or until
golden. Cool and cut into squares.

# BITTERSWEET BROWNIES

*7*hese brownies are just perfect. You can top them with ice cream and pour hot fudge sauce on top.

**Makes about 3 dozen brownies**

Preheat the oven to 350°F. Butter a 9 × 13-inch baking pan.

For the brownies, cream together the butter, sugar, and salt. Add the eggs, one at a time, blending well after each addition. Add the corn syrup (this will make the brownies chewy) and the vanilla. Add the flour, cocoa, and baking powder. Stir in the nuts.

Spread the mixture evenly into the prepared pan and bake for 25 minutes or until the edges are firm but the center is still soft. Cool before frosting.

For the frosting, mix the butter with the chocolate and vanilla. Mix in the powdered sugar, a little at a time. If the frosting becomes too thick, thin it with a little hot water or milk.

Spread over the cooled brownies and cut into 2-inch squares.

## Ingredients

**Brownies**

1 cup (2 sticks) butter, at room temperature

2 cups sugar

1 teaspoon salt

3 eggs

1/4 cup light corn syrup

2 teaspoons vanilla

1 1/2 cups flour

1 cup unsweetened cocoa

1 1/4 teaspoons baking powder

1 cup chopped walnuts or pecans

**Frosting**

3 tablespoons butter, melted

3 ounces unsweetened chocolate, melted and cooled

2 teaspoons vanilla

2 cups powdered sugar

# RICH CHEWY BROWNIES

## Ingredients

6 ounces unsweetened baking chocolate

1 cup (2 sticks) butter, at room temperature

4 large eggs

2 cups sugar

1 tablespoon vanilla

1/2 cup flour

1 cup semisweet chocolate chips (6 ounces)

*I*f there is anything that brings greater comfort than biting into a slightly warm, fresh, chewy brownie, I am not aware of it. These are so wonderful that you should consider making a double batch.

**Makes 1 dozen brownies**

Preheat the oven to 350°F. Butter and flour an 8-inch square pan.

Melt the chocolate and butter together in the microwave, checking and stirring with a wooden spoon every 30 seconds. Stir until smooth and set aside.

Using a mixer, beat the eggs for 5 minutes on high speed until they are thick and lemon-colored. Add sugar and blend on low speed. Add the vanilla and chocolate mixture to the egg mixture and blend on low speed. Add the flour, mixing gently. Pour into the prepared pan and sprinkle with the chocolate chips.

Bake for 45 to 55 minutes, being careful not to overbake. When done, a toothpick inserted into the center should come out almost clean. Remove the pan from the oven and cool. Cut the brownies into squares or bars.

# CRÈME BRÛLÉE

*T*his is known as *crème brûlée* in France and as *flan* in Spanish-speaking countries. By any name, this custard is delicious.

Serves 6

Preheat the oven to 350°F.

In a small, heavy saucepan, melt the caramels and milk together. Or eliminate this step and use a tablespoonful of the apple-dipping caramel you can find in the produce department of your supermarket. Spoon the caramel mixture equally into the bottoms of six 6-ounce custard cups. Or use an 8-inch flan pan or a round baking dish.

Mix all the custard ingredients together. Pour the custard mixture over the caramel. Set the cups or pan in a shallow baking dish. Place the baking dish in the oven and fill with hot water to a depth of 1 inch.

Bake 30 to 40 minutes, or until the center is nearly set. Serve warm or chilled. Just before serving, invert the custard cups onto separate plates (or a platter if you've used a flan pan or baking dish).

*For chocolate flan:* Melt 4 ounces of semi-sweet chocolate and fold the cooled chocolate into the custard mixture before baking.

## Ingredients

**Caramel**

12 caramels

1/4 cup milk

**Custard**

4 eggs

2 cups milk

1/3 cup sugar

Pinch of salt

## Hint

You can spread a mixture of brown sugar and butter on the top of the custard and place it under the broiler until melted—delicious!

# RUM BALLS

## Ingredients

1 pound stale cake or 1 (8-inch) layer of chocolate cake

½ can (1-pound size) chocolate frosting

2 tablespoons rum or rum flavoring

Chocolate coating (recipe follows)

*R*um balls are very popular and are considered a great treat. Most bakeries use stale cake and cookies to create these delicacies. They are always just a bit different depending on the cake, muffins, cookies, or bread you use. Have fun making these.

**Makes 4 dozen rum balls**

Mix the cake, frosting, and rum together. You may need to add a little more frosting to make the dough pliable.

Cover and refrigerate for 1 hour or up to several days.

Shape the dough into small balls and place them on wax paper. Refrigerate them while you prepare the chocolate coating.

Dip the rum balls into the slightly cooled, melted chocolate coating. Use a toothpick, bamboo skewer, or fondue fork to hold the rum ball while dipping. Or drop the rum balls directly into the melted chocolate and remove the balls using a fondue fork.

Set the dipped candies onto wax paper and allow to harden at room temperature.

# CHOCOLATE COATING

## Ingredients

1 pound Chocolate A'Peels
    or artificially flavored
    chocolate, or 1 pound
    semisweet or milk
    chocolate

*T*ry to find a candy-making supply store from which you can buy dipping chocolate. The best product to use for home candy making is the chocolate that contains no cocoa butter. It is called artificially flavored chocolate, but it is difficult to tell the difference when using it for coating candy. If you use real chocolate you will need to temper it and that is painstakingly difficult for a beginner.

If you are melting semisweet chocolate or A'Peels you can use a microwave. Place the chocolate in an 8-cup Pyrex measuring cup. Heat the chocolate for about 2 minutes. Remove the chocolate and stir it until it is smooth.

If you are melting real milk chocolate or white chocolate you will have to use a double boiler. Using a wooden spoon to stir the chocolate will eliminate the possibility of a metallic taste in your candy.

# SUGAR-FREE APPLESAUCE

## Ingredients

10 pounds tart apples
2 cans (12 ounces each)
    sugar-free soda (cherry,
    grape, raspberry, orange,
    or strawberry)
3 tablespoons sugar
    substitute
1 teaspoon cinnamon,
    optional

## Hint

If you cook the apples just to the boiling point, they make a great apple pie filling. By using precooked apples in the pie, the crust will not puff up over the filling.

*T*his is low calorie, healthful, and very comforting. If you can wait for a bumper crop of apples in the fall, choose the tart varieties. This will keep in your refrigerator for several months in a tightly sealed jar.

**Makes 4 quarts**

If you prefer, peel the apples before cooking. Remove the cores and seeds, and cut into wedges or chunks. Place the apples in a large pot. Pour the soda over the apples and stir with a wooden spoon.

Heat the apples and soda to boiling. If you prefer a less crisp applesauce, simmer for 10 minutes. Turn off the heat and cover the pot. After an hour, stir in the sugar substitute. Add more sweetener to taste, or add the cinnamon, if desired.

# BAKED APPLES

*Ingredients*

¹/₄ cup raisins

6 baking apples, cored and
    seeded

1 can (12 ounces) diet soda
    (orange, cherry, grape, or
    raspberry)

Warm cream or milk,
    optional

*T*his is an old recipe for delicious, low-calorie apples. Served warm with cream or even nonfat milk, it is comfort personified.

**Serves 6**

Preheat the oven to 400°F.

Soak the raisins in hot water for 15 minutes and drain. Place the apples in a baking dish and stuff the centers with the raisins. Pour the soda over the apples and bake for 15 minutes. If you prefer a softer apple, bake for a few additional minutes.

# FRUIT COBBLER

2 quarts fresh blackberries,
  blueberries, strawberries
  or raspberries
1½ cups sugar
4 tablespoons tapioca
1 teaspoon vanilla
1 teaspoon lemon juice
1 package lemon cake mix
½ cup (1 stick) butter,
  chopped
Whipping cream or whipped
  topping, optional

*F*un and easy to make after you have been out berry picking.

**Serves 8**

Preheat the oven to 350°F. Butter a 9 × 13-inch baking pan.

Mix together the berries, sugar (use more if the berries are tart), tapioca, vanilla, and lemon juice. Pour this mixture into the prepared pan.

Sprinkle the dry cake mix over the berries and top with chunks of butter. Bake until the cobbler is bubbly. Serve warm with whipped cream or whipped topping.

# CHEESE BLINTZES

*T*hese are actually filled crepes. Serve them hot in a chafing dish and drizzle jam or jelly over the tops of the blintzes. You can also lay well-drained canned fruit between the crepes. Use blueberries, apricots, peaches, or your favorite fruit.

**Serves 8**

*To make cheese filling:* Combine all ingredients in a food processor until smooth and creamy. Set aside.

*To make crepes:* Mix all the ingredients except clarified butter in a blender until smooth. Heat a heavy 6-inch frying pan. Brush the bottom of the pan with clarified butter (page 228), which will not smoke when heated to high temperatures. Pour 1/4 cup of the batter into the heated pan and swirl, making sure the bottom of the pan is covered with the batter. Cook the crepe quickly, turning with your fingertips or a spatula. Cook until the crepe is set but not browned.

Place the crepe on a plate and fill with 1 tablespoon of the cheese filling. Fold on opposite side and then roll up like a jelly roll. Place the blintzes on a plate, seam side down, and refrigerate until cooking time.

To cook, fry the blintzes in clarified butter until well browned, or bake them in the bottom of a buttered baking dish at 425°F for 10 to 15 minutes or until browned.

## Ingredients

**Cheese filling**

1 pound farmer cheese

4 ounces cream cheese, at room temperature

1 egg

1 egg yolk

1/4 cup sugar

1 teaspoon vanilla

Grated peel of one orange

**Crepes**

1 cup flour, sifted

Pinch of salt

2 egg yolks

2 eggs

3/4 cup milk

1/2 cup (1 stick) butter, melted and cooled

Clarified butter

# HOMEMADE VANILLA ICE CREAM

## Ingredients

2 cups milk
4 cups heavy whipping
   cream
1 tablespoon vanilla extract
2 cups sugar
12 egg yolks

*I* have yet to meet someone who doesn't enjoy ice cream. There are lots of wonderful brands to buy for instant gratification, but if you happen to have an ice-cream freezer, then you know that part of the pleasure is making your own. This is the recipe for vanilla, but you can add fruits, chocolate, and nuts for variety.

**Makes 2 quarts**

Scald the milk, 1½ cups of cream, and the vanilla together. Add 1 cup sugar to the milk mixture and bring to a boil, stirring constantly.

Beat the egg yolks with the remaining sugar until thick and lemon colored. Add about 1 cup of the hot cream mixture to the eggs, then slowly stir all of the egg mixture into the hot cream mixture. Return to heat and stir to thicken. *Do not boil.*

Cover and chill the mixture. Process in an ice-cream maker according to the manufacturer's directions. Freeze.

## Hint

Your ice cream freezer will have instructions and recipes but here are a few tricks for making perfect ice cream:

- Fast freezing results in smooth, fine-textured ice cream. If you use the freezer section of your refrigerator, set it on the coldest temperature possible. Fast freezing also prevents the formation of ice crystals.
- Homemade ice cream needs to be eaten as soon as it is made because it does not keep well. That's the fun of making your own.
- You should try to get manufactured whipping cream that contains up to 48 percent butterfat from a local dairy. High fat is another secret to smooth, delicious ice cream.
- With the right equipment and some imagination, it's almost impossible to make bad ice cream.

# SHERBET

## Ingredients

1 cup fruit

1/2 cup fruit juice, such as
    unsweetened apple juice

2 tablespoons honey

4 tablespoons lemon juice

2 egg whites, at room
    temperature

*T*his recipe is for basic sherbet that you can make in your freezer. Perfect for someone with a sore throat. Experiment with flavors—I have used peaches, pears, melon, berries, and canned and fresh pineapple.

**Makes 1 quart**

In a blender, mix together the fruit, juice, honey, and lemon juice to make a purée.

Whip the egg whites until they form soft peaks. Fold into the fruit purée. Cover and freeze.

# CAKE AND ICE CREAM WITH HOT FUDGE SAUCE

*T*his was served 50 years ago as one of the favorite desserts at Sanders' Ice Cream Parlor in Detroit, Michigan.

**Serves 12**

Bake the cake mix in a 9 × 13-inch baking pan according to the package directions.

Cool the cake completely. Remove the cake from the pan and cut it into 24 squares.

Slice the ice-cream block into 12 slices. Place 1 slice of ice cream on top of 12 of the cake squares. Cover the ice cream with another square of cake. Press down on top of the second layer of cake. Freeze the ice cream–cake squares until serving time.

Place cake squares on individual serving plates and allow to sit for 10 minutes. Heat the fudge sauce and pour it over each serving. Top with whipped cream or whipped topping if desired. Serve immediately.

## Ingredients

1 package dark chocolate cake mix

1 quart ice-cream block

2 cups bittersweet hot fudge sauce (page 290)

Whipped cream or whipped topping, optional

# BANANA SPLIT

## Ingredients

1 banana, peeled and sliced
   lengthwise
1 scoop vanilla ice cream
1 scoop chocolate ice cream
1 scoop strawberry ice
   cream
2 tablespoons crushed
   pineapple
2 tablespoons frozen strawberries, defrosted
2 tablespoons bittersweet
   hot fudge sauce (page
   290)
Whipped cream
Chopped peanuts
3 long-stemmed cherries

## Hint

You can use any flavors of
ice cream you like and any
flavor toppings. You can use
tall soda glasses and cut the
bananas in slices and pile
the ice cream and toppings
on top of each other.

*T*his is the most decadent ice-cream dessert in
the world. Someone who really loves sweets will
take great comfort in this.

**Serves 1**

If you don't have banana split bowls or crepe
dishes, use a wide, shallow soup bowl. Lay the
bananas slices on their sides and place the three
scoops of ice cream side by side on top of the
banana.

Use the pineapple, strawberries, and hot
fudge sauce as toppings—each on a different
scoop of ice cream. Garnish with whipped
cream, chopped nuts, and cherries.

# PEANUT BUTTER TIN ROOF SUNDAE

*I* served this at our dessert parlor—mostly, I think, to myself.

**Serves 1**

## Ingredients

2 generous scoops French vanilla ice cream

4 tablespoons chunky peanut butter

4 tablespoons bittersweet hot fudge sauce (page 290)

Whipped cream

Chopped peanuts

1 long-stemmed cherry

Use a sundae glass or a big goblet. Pour 2 tablespoons of hot fudge sauce into the bottom of the glass. Pile in the ice cream, layered with the peanut butter and remaining hot fudge sauce. Garnish with whipped cream, chopped nuts, and a cherry.

# STRAWBERRY SHORTCAKE

## Ingredients

**Shortcake**

4 tablespoons (½ stick)
  butter, at room
  temperature
1 cup sugar
3 eggs
1½ cups flour
2 teaspoons baking powder
¼ cup milk

**Topping**

3 cups fresh strawberries,
  or frozen, defrosted
½ cup granulated sugar
1 cup heavy whipping
  cream
2 tablespoons powdered
  sugar
½ teaspoon vanilla

*A*nother big-time favorite. You can use sponge cake, angel food cake, the little individual shortcakes that come packaged in the produce department of your supermarket, or make your own.

**Serves 4**

Preheat the oven to 350°F. Butter a 9-inch square baking pan.

For the shortcake, cream together the butter and sugar and add the eggs, one at a time, beating well after each addition. Add the flour, baking powder, and milk and beat until just mixed.

Pour the batter into the prepared pan and bake for 30 minutes or until a toothpick inserted into the center comes out clean.

For the topic, reserve 4 whole berries for garnish. Mash half of the remaining strawberries and slice the rest. Add the granulated sugar to the mashed and sliced strawberries and toss gently. Refrigerate for several hours.

Whip the cream until foamy and add the powdered sugar. Beat until stiff. Add the vanilla.

To assemble: Cut the shortcake into 4 large squares and place each square, bottom side up, on a dessert plate. Top the cake with the sliced strawberries and pour the strawberry juice over the cake. Garnish with whipped cream and a whole strawberry.

## Hint

You can use raspberries, blackberries, or cherries in place of the strawberries.

# BREAD PUDDING

## Ingredients

6 eggs, beaten well

1 cup sugar

2 cups light cream

½ cup (1 stick) butter, melted

1 tablespoon vanilla

1 large loaf French bread or egg bread, broken into pieces

1 teaspoon cinnamon

1 cup crushed pineapple

1 cup raisins, soaked in hot water for 15 minutes and drained

1 jar (16½ ounces) Bing cherries, drained, optional

*B*read pudding is old-fashioned, but almost at the top of the comfort foods list. It's a fabulous way to get rid of stale bread and is elegant enough to serve at a brunch or a potluck dinner. It seems to make everyone happy.

**Serves 12**

Preheat the oven to 350°F and butter a 9 × 13-inch baking pan or a large ceramic baking dish.

Beat the eggs with the sugar, cream, butter, and vanilla and pour this mixture over the bread cubes. Stir until the bread is moistened. Stir the cinnamon into this mixture and add the pineapple and raisins. Stir in the cherries if you are using them.

Spoon the mixture into the prepared pan. Bake for 30 to 40 minutes or until the pudding is set. Serve hot. Pass cream to pour over the pudding.

# FUDGE BREAD PUDDING

*T*ake this to a potluck and you'll be the star of the show!

**Serves 12**

Preheat the oven to 325°F. Butter and flour a 6-cup baking dish.

Combine the chocolate, butter, and sugar in a saucepan and cook over low heat, stirring constantly, until everything is melted together. Stir until smooth; set aside to cool. Add the cream.

Whisk in the eggs and vanilla; fold in the bread. Pour into the prepared pan. Place the pan in a larger pan and put both in the oven. Pour 2 inches of hot water into the larger pan and bake for 40 minutes, or until the pudding is firm in the center.

Serve warm with vanilla ice cream or whipped topping.

## Ingredients

1 package (12 ounces) semisweet chocolate chips, or 10 ounces semisweet chocolate

½ cup (1 stick) butter

½ cup sugar

2 cups light cream

4 eggs, well beaten

1 tablespoon vanilla

8 slices white or egg bread, torn into cubes

# BITTERSWEET CHOCOLATE PUDDING

## Ingredients

1½ cups sugar

1 teaspoon salt

⅓ cup cornstarch

1 cup unsweetened cocoa

3 cups evaporated milk

3 cups water

3 eggs, well beaten

2 tablespoons vanilla
     extract

3 tablespoons butter

*T*his is melt-in-your-mouth smooth, comforting, and delicious. The packaged stuff doesn't come close.

**Serves 8**

In a large saucepan, mix together the sugar, salt, cornstarch, and cocoa. Add the milk, water, and eggs. Cook over low heat, stirring constantly, until the mixture thickens.

Remove the mixture from the heat and beat in the vanilla and butter. Cool and serve.

# HOT RICE PUDDING

*T*his is as close as I can get to the marvelous rice pudding I had at Ratners' Restaurant on the lower east side of Manhattan. You can add vanilla, nutmeg, or cinnamon, but it's delicious plain. The bottom is creamy rice and the top is custard.

**Serves 6**

## Ingredients

4 eggs
½ cup sugar
1 teaspoon vanilla
Pinch of salt
1 cup light cream
2 cups milk
1½ cups cooked rice
1 pint heavy cream

Preheat the oven to 350°F. Butter an 8-inch square glass baking dish or a 2-quart casserole.

Beat the eggs and sugar together and add the vanilla, salt, cream, milk, and rice. Pour the mixture into the prepared pan and bake for 1 hour and 15 minutes or until the pudding is set and is golden brown on the top.

Serve warm with heavy cream poured on the top.

# APPLE PIE

## Ingredients

1 cup sugar plus 1 table-
   spoon for the top
4 tablespoons (1/2 stick)
   butter
1/4 cup flour
2 tablespoons water
8 cups tart apples, peeled,
   cored, and sliced
1 1/2 teaspoons cinnamon
1 teaspoon nutmeg
1/2 teaspoon allspice
1/2 teaspoon salt
2 unbaked 9-inch pie crusts

## Hint

You can prepare several of
these pies at the same time
and freeze the pies for up
to 6 months.

*T*he all-American dessert that everyone loves. This makes a deep-dish apple pie. By cooking the apples first, you eliminate the possibility of a big air pocket forming in the middle of the baked pie.

**Serves 6 to 8**

Preheat the oven to 425°F.

Combine 1 cup sugar and the butter in a deep pot and cook over low heat until the mixture starts to bubble. Add the flour and stir until blended. Slowly add the water and apples and cook over low heat, uncovered, until the apples are almost tender, about 5 minutes. *Do not over-cook.* Add the cinnamon, nutmeg, allspice, and salt. Cool the mixture for 30 minutes.

Fill the bottom pie crust with the apple mixture and place the other pie crust on top. Trim and flute the edges. Sprinkle the top pie crust with 1 tablespoon sugar. Bake for 10 minutes. Reduce the oven temperature to 325°F and continue to bake for 45 minutes or until the pie is golden.

# RHUBARB STRAWBERRY PIE

*B*ob Brenman, this pie is for you. If you like this pie tart, use less sugar.

**Serves 6 to 8**

Preheat the oven to 425°F.

In a deep pot, combine 2 cups sugar and the butter and cook over low heat until bubbly. Blend in the flour, cinnamon, allspice, salt, and nutmeg. Add the rhubarb and water and cook until the mixture is thick and the rhubarb is tender, about 10 minutes.

Remove the mixture from the heat and fold in the strawberries. Fill the bottom crust with the rhubarb mixture and put the top crust over the filling. Trim and flute the edges. Sprinkle 1 tablespoon sugar on the top crust.

Bake for 15 minutes and then lower the oven temperature to 325°F and bake for an additional 45 minutes or until the pie is golden brown.

## Ingredients

2 cups sugar plus 1 tablespoon for the top

3 tablespoons butter

1/4 cup flour

1 teaspoon cinnamon

1 teaspoon allspice

Dash of salt

Dash of nutmeg

5 cups fresh rhubarb, chopped

2 tablespoons water

5 cups fresh strawberries, sliced

2 unbaked 9-inch pie crusts

# BANANA CREAM CUSTARD PIE

## Ingredients

3 cups milk

4 egg yolks, well beaten

2/3 cup sugar

1/2 teaspoon salt

1/4 cup cornstarch

1 package (8 ounces) cream
cheese, softened

1/2 cup any finely chopped
nuts

1 teaspoon vanilla

1 tablespoon butter

2 large bananas, sliced

1 baked 9-inch pie crust

1 cup toasted shredded
coconut

*If* you love custard, you'll adore this pie.

**Serves 6 to 8**

Combine the milk, egg yolks, sugar, salt, and cornstarch and cook over low heat. Bring to a boil. Add the cream cheese and stir until the cheese is melted.

Remove the mixture from the heat and add nuts, vanilla, and butter. Stir until well mixed. Cool for 20 to 30 minutes. Place a sheet of plastic wrap on top of the cooling pot to help avoid a crust forming on the custard.

Place the sliced bananas on the bottom of the pie crust and top with the cooled custard. Sprinkle with coconut and refrigerate.

# LEMON MERINGUE PIE

*A*nother classic favorite.

**Serves 6 to 8**

For the filling, mix together the sugar and cornstarch in a saucepan. Slowly stir in the water until well mixed. Stir in the egg yolks. Cook over medium heat until the mixture boils, stirring constantly. Boil for 1 minute and remove from heat. Stir in the lemon juice, grated lemon peel, and butter. Spoon hot filling into the pie crust.

Preheat the oven to 375°F. To prepare the meringue, combine the cream of tartar and egg whites. Use a mixer and beat until soft peaks form. Add the sugar and continue to beat until the meringue is thick and stiff. Heap the meringue onto the cooled pie filling and smooth the meringue to the very edge of the pie. Swirl the meringue toward the center of the pie.

Bake for 10 minutes or until the meringue is golden. Refrigerate until serving.

## Ingredients

**Filling**

1 cup sugar
1/4 cup cornstarch
1 1/2 cups cold water
3 egg yolks, slightly beaten
1/4 cup lemon juice
Grated peel of 1 lemon
1 tablespoon butter
1 baked 9-inch pie crust

**Meringue**

1/2 teaspoon cream of tartar
3 egg whites
1/3 cup sugar

# MILK CHOCOLATE PIE

## Ingredients

2¼ cups milk

1 bar (10 ounces) milk
   chocolate

1 tablespoon flour

1 tablespoon cornstarch

2 egg yolks, well beaten

1 tablespoon butter

1 teaspoon vanilla

1 baked 9-inch pie shell

1 container (12 ounces)
   whipped topping

*A*mericans love milk chocolate. I refer to those who love dark chocolate as gourmets, and lovers of milk chocolate as gourmoos. This recipe is from a 1960 *Sunset* magazine contributor. It's quite sweet and makes a great comfort food.

**Serves 6 to 8**

Scald 2 cups of the milk in the top of a double boiler over hot water. Chop the milk chocolate into bits and stir it into the hot milk until it is melted.

Mix the flour and cornstarch with the remaining ¼ cup milk and stir until smooth. Stir the flour mixture into the milk mixture and stir until thickened. Stir some of the hot mixture into the egg yolks and add this to the chocolate mixture. Stir until smooth.

Remove the mixture from the heat and stir in the butter and the vanilla. Cool the mixture and pour it into the prepared pie shell. Cover the chocolate with whipped cream or whipped topping. Chill until serving.

# SWEET POTATO PIE

*S*imilar in taste and texture to pumpkin pie, this is fun to serve.

**Serves 8 to 12**

Preheat the oven to 350°F and put the crust in either a 10-inch tart pan with a removable bottom or a 10-inch pie pan. Prick the crust with a fork. Bake the pie crust 8 to 10 minutes and set aside to cool.

Using a mixer, combine the sweet potatoes, cream, milk, sugar, eggs, 1/3 cup bourbon, melted butter, cinnamon, and salt. Beat until well blended and pour into the baked crust.

Bake 50 minutes or until a knife inserted in the center of the pie comes out clean. Cool to room temperature.

Combine the brown sugar, 6 tablespoons butter, ginger, and 1 tablespoon bourbon; stir until well mixed. Stir in the chopped pecans and spoon evenly over the top of the pie. Arrange pecan halves around the edges of the pie.

Preheat the broiler. Place the pie on an ungreased cookie sheet 6 to 8 inches under a hot broiler. Cover the edges of the crust with foil to prevent burning. Broil for a minute or two, or until the topping is bubbling. Cool to room temperature and refrigerate until served.

## Ingredients

1 unbaked 10-inch pie crust

3 cups cooked sweet potatoes or yams, fresh or canned

3/4 cup whipping cream

1/2 cup milk

1/2 cup sugar

3 eggs, slightly beaten

1/3 cup plus 1 tablespoon bourbon

1 tablespoon butter, melted

1 teaspoon cinnamon

Pinch of salt

1/2 cup firmly packed brown sugar

6 tablespoons (3/4 stick) butter, at room temperature

2 tablespoons ginger

1/2 cup chopped pecans

18 pecan halves

# MISSISSIPPI MUD PIE

## Ingredients

1 quart coffee ice cream
1 prepared 9-inch choco-
    late cookie crust
1 cup caramel or butter-
    scotch topping
1 cup fudge sauce
Whipped cream or
    whipped topping,
    optional

## Hint

If you want to make your
own cookie crust, try the
one in the Kahlúa pie
recipe (page 281).

*A* fast and easy dessert to make and one that
everyone loves.

**Serves 6 to 8**

Spoon the ice cream into the prepared crust
and press the ice cream down firmly. Freeze for
15 minutes. Spoon caramel sauce on top of the
ice cream and return pie to the freezer for 15
minutes. Spoon hot fudge sauce over the top of
the entire pie. Freeze the pie until serving time.
(This can be stored for at least a month.) Remove the pie from the freezer 15 to 30 minutes
before serving. Decorate the top with whipped
cream or whipped topping.

# KAHLÚA PIE

*T*his dessert was the favorite at Chocoholics Dessert Parlor in Arcata, Calif. It can be eaten frozen, at room temperature, or refrigerated. Use a prepared chocolate cookie crumb crust if you prefer, but here is how to make it yourself.

**Serves 8 to 12**

Preheat the oven to 350°F.

Combine all of the crust ingredients and blend well. Butter a 10-inch pie pan and press the mixture onto the sides and bottom of the pan using your moistened fingertips. Bake crust 10 minutes, or until brown.

To make the filling, beat the butter until very creamy. Add the sugar and continue beating until light and fluffy. Add the chocolate and instant coffee and beat well. Add the eggs, one at a time, beating well after each addition. Mix on high until the mixture is very thick and fluffy. Pour the filling into the cooled pie shell and refrigerate, covered, for at least 12 hours.

To make the topping, whip the cream until almost stiff. Add the powdered sugar, coffee, and liqueur. Spread or pipe the cream over the filling using a pastry tube so that the whipped cream topping is very high. Garnish with chocolate curls or chocolate coffee beans. Refrigerate for several hours, or freeze for as long as 6 weeks. Serve frozen or chilled.

## Ingredients

**Chocolate crumb crust**

1½ cups flour
½ cup (1 stick) butter, at room temperature
¼ cup firmly packed brown sugar
¾ cup chopped pecans
1 ounce unsweetened chocolate, grated
1 teaspoon vanilla
1 tablespoon water

**Filling**

¾ cup (1½ sticks) butter, at room temperature
1 cup extra-fine sugar
1½ ounces unsweetened chocolate, melted and cooled
1 tablespoon instant coffee
3 eggs

**Topping**

2 cups whipping cream
½ cup powdered sugar
2 tablespoons instant coffee
2 tablespoons Kahlúa, or any coffee-flavored liqueur
Chocolate curls or chocolate coffee beans for garnish

# KEY LIME PIE

## Ingredients

½ cup lime juice

1 can (14 ounces) sweet-
ened condensed milk

2 tablespoons grated lime
peel

4 eggs, separated

1 baked 8-inch pie crust

½ teaspoon cream of tartar

⅓ cup sugar

*O*ne of America's most treasured pies, Key lime pie is very easy to prepare. If you use individual pie pans, pile the meringue on high and sprinkle with flaked coconut.

**Serves 8**

Preheat the oven to 350°F.

Combine the lime juice, condensed milk, lime peel, and egg yolks (reserve whites); stir until smooth. Pour the mixture into the prepared crust.

Beat the egg whites until foamy; add cream of tartar and sugar and beat until stiff. Spread the meringue on top of the pie and bake 10 minutes, or until the meringue is golden. Refrigerate until served.

# EASY PECAN PIE

*E*asy and very delicious. Use your favorite unbaked pie crust.

**Serves 8**

## Ingredients

3 eggs, slightly beaten
1 cup dark corn syrup
1 cup sugar
Pinch of salt
2 tablespoons butter,
   melted
1 teaspoon vanilla
1 cup whole pecans
1 unbaked 10-inch pie crust

Preheat the oven to 400°F.

Combine all of the ingredients except the crust and stir until smooth. Pour the mixture into the unbaked crust. Bake 15 minutes. Lower the oven temperature to 350°F and bake an additional 35 minutes, or until a knife comes out clean when inserted in the center of the pie.

## Hint

For chocolate pecan pie, add 2 ounces of melted and cooled bittersweet or semisweet chocolate, or 4 tablespoons cocoa and 1 tablespoon melted butter to the batter.

# SIMPLE SYRUP

## Ingredients

1 cup sugar
1 cup white corn syrup or
    dextrose
1 cup water

## Hint

If you are in a hurry, boil
together 1 cup of sugar and
1 cup of water and use it as
soon as it is cool. This mixture will not keep but will
form beautiful rock sugar
crystals after a few days.

*T*his syrup will enhance your cakes and keep
them fresh and moist to the last bite. Fill a spray
bottle with simple syrup and lightly mist the
cooled layers of a cake before frosting. It keeps
for several months in a tightly covered container
and doesn't need to be refrigerated.

**Makes 2 cups**

Combine all of the ingredients in a saucepan
and bring them to a full boil. Cool before using.

# LEMON CURD

This recipe was given to me by my friend Lolita Leen. Lemon curd is one of my favorite comfort foods. It is thick and tart and tastes like the best lemon pie filling in the world. It is expensive to buy, but very simple to make. Using your imagination you can create some fabulous treats. Mixed with an equal portion of whipped cream it can be used as a filling for tarts and pies.

**Makes 3 cups**

In a double boiler, melt the butter and stir in the lemon juice, lemon peel, sugar, and salt. Slightly beat the egg yolks together with the whole eggs and add this to the butter mixture.

Cook the mixture over medium heat for about 30 minutes and use a wire whisk to stir until thickened. You can use a heavy saucepan, but the lemon curd tends to scorch easily.

## Ingredients

½ cup (1 stick) butter, at room temperature

½ cup fresh lemon juice (about 3 lemons)

Grated peel of 1 large lemon

1½ cups sugar

Pinch of salt

3 egg yolks

3 large eggs

## Hint

You can replace the fresh lemon juice with bottled lemon juice. If you use a fresh lemon, roll the lemon on your counter until it is soft. You'll get more juice.

In order to simplify grating the lemon peel, freeze the already squeezed lemon rind for 30 minutes.

If tightly covered and refrigerated, lemon curd will keep for several months.

# MICROWAVE LEMON CURD

## Ingredients

¹/₂ cup (1 stick) butter

3 large eggs, beaten

1 cup sugar

¹/₂ cup lemon juice

1 teaspoon grated lemon peel

*A*nother gem from Merrill Lipowsky.

**Makes 2 cups**

Melt the butter in the microwave. Whisk together the eggs, sugar, lemon juice, and lemon peel in a 4-cup Pyrex measuring cup. Add the melted butter and stir until smooth. Microwave for 2 minutes and stir the mixture. If necessary, microwave for another minute or two until the mixture is thick.

Cover the lemon curd with plastic wrap and allow it to cool to room temperature. Stored in a tightly sealed jar in the refrigerator, this should keep for several weeks.

# WHIPPED CREAM FROSTING

## Ingredients

2 cups whipping cream
¼ cup powdered sugar

*W*hipped cream frosting delights everyone, even people who don't like frosting. It's easy to prepare and although it needs to be kept refrigerated until it is served, it holds up surprisingly well at room temperature.

I freeze wedding cakes with whipped cream frosting for at least an hour so they will hold up for several hours during the wedding reception. You can freeze decorated cake layers longer if you like, but remember it will take longer to defrost at room temperature, so plan accordingly.

**Makes 4 cups**

Whip the cream until it is frothy and add the sugar slowly. Beat until stiff and use immediately to frost the sides and top of one 8-inch, 2-layer cake.

# CREAM CHEESE FROSTING

## Ingredients

1 package (8 ounces)
   cream cheese, at room
   temperature
4 tablespoons (½ stick)
   butter, at room
   temperature
2 cups powdered sugar
1 tablespoon lemon juice or
   extract
1 teaspoon vanilla

*T*his is a lovely creamy frosting—perfect on carrot and zucchini cakes. It also works well as a wedding cake frosting.

**Makes 2 cups**

Blend all of the ingredients together until light and creamy. Scrape down the sides and bottom of the mixing bowl so no clumps of cheese remain. Spread the frosting between the layers and on the top and sides of the cake. Garnish with nuts, fruit, or flowers.

*For chocolate cream cheese frosting:* Eliminate the lemon extract. Melt and cool 4 ounces of semisweet chocolate and blend the chocolate into the frosting. Easy and delicious.

*For bittersweet chocolate frosting:* Use 2 ounces of unsweetened chocolate, melted and cooled, and blend into the frosting.

# CHOCOLATE MOUSSE FROSTING

This frosting is rich and creamy, not too sweet, and very simple to prepare. It is also spectacular served as mousse in tall glasses.

**Makes 3 cups**

Beat together the chocolate and the condensed milk. Gradually add the water and instant pudding; mix until smooth. Fold in the whipped cream. Use it as cake frosting immediately, or spoon it into six fluted glasses and chill for at least 1 hour before serving as mousse.

## *Ingredients*

2 ounces unsweetened chocolate, melted and cooled

1 can (14 ounces) sweetened condensed milk

½ cup cold water

1 package (3 ounces) instant chocolate pudding

1 cup heavy cream, whipped

## *Hint*

Whip the cream before you melt the chocolate. Scrape the whipped cream into a bowl and use the original bowl in which you whipped the cream to complete the frosting. There's no need to wash the beater and bowl in between.

# BITTERSWEET HOT FUDGE SAUCE

## Ingredients

1 cup heavy cream
6 tablespoons (3/4 stick) unsalted butter, cut into
  cubes
2/3 cup sugar
2/3 cup dark brown sugar,
  tightly packed
Pinch of salt
1 cup cocoa

## Hint

Sift or strain the cocoa
before adding it to the
cream-sugar mixture so
there are no lumps. If you
have lumpy fudge sauce, it
still tastes fabulous.

*T*his recipe is worth the price of this book. We made a jillion gallons of this wonderful, thick, dark, and delicious sauce for our dessert parlor. The only difference is that we used a cocoa that was specially designed for our use, but you will still come close to perfection with a good grade of cocoa available at a well-stocked supermarket or gourmet store. Heat this sauce and pour it over ice cream and it becomes thick and chewy. Pure comfort for lovers of hot fudge.

**Makes 2 cups**

Heat the cream and butter over medium heat until the mixture starts to boil. Add the sugars and salt and cook until the sugars are dissolved.

Reduce the heat and stir in the cocoa. Mix until there are no lumps of cocoa remaining. Serve immediately or refrigerate and store for up to several months. Microwave the sauce for 1 minute or until liquid enough to pour, but be careful not to overheat and burn the sauce.

# CHOCOLATE TURTLE CHEESECAKE

*7his* cheesecake is pure, sweet comfort. Eating it is a sensual delight.

**Serves 12 to 18**

Preheat the oven to 350°F. Butter a 9-inch springform pan. Combine the wafer crumbs and butter and press into the bottom of the buttered pan. Place the pan on an ungreased cookie sheet and bake 10 minutes. Remove the pan from the oven and cool. Keep the oven on.

Using the top of a double boiler, melt the caramels and the evaporated milk. Stir until smooth. Pour the caramel mixture over the prepared crust. Top with chopped pecans.

Combine the cream cheese, sugar, and vanilla and beat together until well blended, making sure to scrape down the bowl several times. Add the eggs, one at a time, beating until just mixed. Stir in the melted chocolate and pour the cream cheese mixture over the caramel and pecans.

Bake 40 minutes or until set. Chill overnight before serving.

## Ingredients

**Vanilla crumb crust**

2 cups vanilla wafer crumbs
6 tablespoons (3/4 stick) butter, melted

**Caramel filling**

1 bag (14 ounces) caramels, unwrapped
1 can (5 ounces) evaporated milk
1 cup chopped pecans
3 packages (8 ounces each) cream cheese, at room temperature
1/2 cup sugar
1 teaspoon vanilla
2 eggs
1/2 cup semisweet chocolate chips, melted

# VERY RICH CHEESECAKE

## Ingredients

1½ cups finely ground
   toasted almonds
4 packages (8 ounces each)
   cream cheese, at room
   temperature
1½ cups sugar
1 pint (8 ounces) sour
   cream
1 tablespoon vanilla
2 tablespoons fresh lemon
   juice
6 large eggs

*T*his is a five-star restaurant cheesecake, easy to prepare and marvelous to serve. You can vary the flavorings and even the crust and always be assured of a great dessert.

**Serves 12 to 18**

Preheat the oven to 325°F. Butter a 9-inch springform pan and sprinkle ½ cup of the almonds into the bottom of the pan.

Cream the cheese until it is very smooth. Make sure there are no lumps in the bottom of the mixing bowl. Add the sugar and continue beating until the mixture is light and fluffy. Add the sour cream, vanilla, and lemon juice. Add the eggs, one at a time, being careful not to overbeat. Stir in the remaining 1 cup of almonds by hand. Pour the batter into the prepared pan.

Place the cheesecake on a cookie sheet covered with foil in the center of your oven and bake 45 to 60 minutes, or until set. Let the cheesecake rest in the oven with the heat turned off for 1 hour. Keep the door slightly open. Refrigerate the baked cheesecake for at least 4 hours before decorating and serving.

*For German chocolate cheesecake:* Fold 4 ounces of melted and cooled sweet chocolate or milk chocolate into the batter. Add 1/4 cup heavy cream or sour cream. After the cheesecake is baked and cooled, spread coconut pecan frosting over the top. Decorate the frosted cheesecake with pecan halves. Tube chocolate decorations around the top border. Refrigerate until served.

*For Kahlúa cheesecake:* Add 4 ounces of melted and cooled unsweetened chocolate to the batter plus 1/4 cup coffee-flavored liqueur or very strong coffee. After the cheesecake is baked and cooled, spread sweetened whipped cream over the top and decorate with candy or real coffee beans. Refrigerate until served.

*For rum pumpkin cheesecake:* Substitute firmly packed brown sugar for the white sugar. Add 1 cup of cooked or canned mashed pumpkin, 1 tablespoon cinnamon, 1 tablespoon ginger, 2 tablespoons rum or rum flavoring, 1 teaspoon allspice, and 1 teaspoon nutmeg to the batter. After the cheesecake is baked and cooled, spread sweetened whipped cream over the top. Sprinkle cinnamon and sugar lightly over the whipped cream. Refrigerate until served.

# OH! CHOCOLATE!

## Ingredients

5 tablespoons sweet butter

1 pound semisweet chocolate, such as Callebaut, melted and cooled

4 eggs

1 tablespoon sugar

1 tablespoon flour

*A* totally decadent cake—only about 2 inches tall but almost solid chocolate. It contains only a tiny amount of flour so it can be consumed by people allergic to flour. It is pure comfort to a dedicated chocoholic.

This is an expensive cake because you *must* use the very finest chocolate available: Callebaut from Belgium.

**Serves 12**

Preheat the oven to 425°F. Cut a round of parchment to fit into the bottom of a heavily buttered 8-inch cake pan.

Melt the butter and chocolate together in a microwave until the mixture is shiny and smooth. Set aside to cool.

Place the eggs and sugar in a mixer bowl. Place the bowl over boiling water and whisk the eggs with a wire whip until they are skin temperature or 98°F. Don't overheat or you will have coddled eggs. Remove the egg mixture from the heat and beat on high speed for 15 minutes, until the eggs are very thick and lemon colored.

Carefully fold in the flour. Gently fold into the chocolate mixture. I find the side of my hand is the best tool I own for this job. Pour the batter into the prepared cake pan and bake for exactly

15 minutes. Remove cake from the oven to cool. When cool, place it in the freezer—pan and all—for at least 12 hours.

On serving day, remove cake from the freezer. Remove the cake from the pan and place on a serving plate. (If you have trouble removing it from the pan, place it in a hot oven for 2 minutes.) Decorate the sides and top of the cake with chocolate frosting, chocolate glaze, or a dab of whipped cream and raspberries.

# SUPER-MOIST CHOCOLATE CAKE

## Ingredients

1 cup mayonnaise

2 cups sugar

4 eggs

1 teaspoon vanilla

2 cups flour

1 cup unsweetened cocoa

1¾ teaspoons baking soda

⅓ cup milk

1 cup water

1 cup (6 ounces) semisweet
chocolate chips

*T*his is perfect when you need the comfort of a quick chocolate cake. Use the real mayonnaise for the best results—lowfat and fat-free won't work.

**Serves 18**

Preheat the oven to 350°F. Butter and flour a 9 × 13-inch pan.

Cream together the mayonnaise, sugar, eggs, and vanilla. Add the flour, cocoa, and baking soda and stir to blend. Add the milk and water and beat 2 minutes. Fold in the chocolate chips.

Bake 30 minutes, or until cake tests done. Cool. Sprinkle with powdered sugar or frost with chocolate frosting if desired.

# LEMON POPPY SEED POUND CAKE

*T*his is one of my personal favorite comfort foods even though it's not chocolate. It is a moist, melt-in-your-mouth cake and as close to perfection as possible.

**Serves 12 to 18**

Soak the poppy seeds in the water for 15 minutes.

Preheat the oven to 350°F and spray a Bundt pan with nonstick cooking spray. Dust lightly with flour.

Combine all of the ingredients, including the poppy seeds, and beat until smooth, about 2 minutes. Pour into the prepared pan and bake 40 minutes, or until cake tests done.

Remove the cake from the oven and place the pan on a slightly damp dish towel until almost cool. This will prevent the cake from sinking. When it is completely cooled, invert the cake onto a cake platter. Serve with lemon curd (page 285), whipped cream, or fresh fruit. This is living!

## Ingredients

2 tablespoons poppy seeds

3/4 cup water

1 box lemon cake mix

1 box (3 1/8 ounces) lemon instant pudding

1 tablespoon lemon extract

3/4 cup sour cream

1/3 cup vegetable or canola oil

3 eggs

# CARROT CAKE

## Ingredients

2 cups unsifted flour

2 cups sugar, or 1½ cups
fructose

2 teaspoons baking soda

1 teaspoon salt

3 teaspoons cinnamon

4 eggs

1 cup corn oil

4 cups (8 or 9) finely grated
carrots

1 cup raisins, soaked in hot
water 10 minutes and
drained

1 cup finely chopped
walnuts, almonds,
pecans, or hazelnuts

## Hint

Diabetics can replace the
sugar with fructose. Fructose does not go directly
into the bloodstream but is
stored in the liver as glyco-
gen. If you use fructose and
you are preparing carrot
cake for a diabetic child, I
suggest you bake tiny muffins that can be included in
their diet. Reduce raisins to
¼ cup and serve cake un-
frosted.

*T*his carrot cake is moist and delicious. This
recipe also makes a great loaf cake and is fabulous for muffins.

Serves 18 to 24

Preheat the oven to 350°F. Butter and flour
three 8-inch cake pans (yes, three) and dust
lightly with flour.

Mix together the flour, sugar, baking soda,
salt, and cinnamon and set aside. Beat the eggs
with a mixer until very light and creamy. Beat in
the oil gradually. Add the flour mixture and beat
until smooth. Stir in the carrots, raisins, and
nuts.

Pour the batter into prepared pans and bake
30 minutes or until the cakes test done. Cool for
15 minutes. Remove the cakes from their pans
and continue cooling on a wire cake rack.

Freeze the layers until they are easy to handle. These layers freeze very well for a long time.

Frost the cake with cream cheese frosting
(page 288) or whipped cream.

# MOIST AND CREAMY BANANA CAKE

*A*nother very old cake recipe, this was given to me when my daughter was born and is her very favorite cake. It's moist and delicious. This recipe also makes marvelous muffins and banana bread.

**Serves 12 to 18**

Preheat the oven to 350°F. Butter two 8-inch cake pans and dust lightly with flour.

Cream together the butter and sugar. Add the eggs and bananas and mix. In a separate bowl, blend the flour, baking soda, and salt. Add the dry ingredients and buttermilk alternately to the banana mixture. Beat until smooth. Add the nuts and raisins or dates, if desired.

Bake 30 minutes, or until the cake tests done. (This is a dense and heavy cake. Make sure it is thoroughly baked before removing it from the oven.) Remove the cake from oven and place the pan on a slightly damp tea towel to cool (this will prevent the layers from sinking).

Let the cake cool. Dust the layers with powdered sugar, or frost with chocolate frosting or whipped cream.

## Ingredients

1/2 cup (1 stick) butter, at room temperature

1 3/4 cups sugar

3 large eggs

4 very ripe bananas

2 1/2 cups flour

1 tablespoon baking soda

Pinch of salt

2/3 cup buttermilk

1/2 cup chopped nuts, optional

1/4 cup chopped raisins or dates, optional

# APPLE CHUNK CAKE

1½ cups vegetable or
   canola oil

2 cups sugar

3 large eggs

3 cups flour

Pinch of salt

1 teaspoon baking soda

6 Granny Smith apples,
   peeled, cored, and cut
   into cubes

2 cups chopped pecans

1 tablespoon vanilla or
   maple extract

1 can (16 ounces) lemon or
   vanilla frosting, optional

Pecan halves for garnish,
   optional

*T*his is an absolutely wonderful cake, especially if you use tart apples. It is a very moist cake that stays fresh for a week and doesn't require frosting.

**Serves 12 to 18**

Preheat the oven to 350°F. Spray a Bundt pan with nonstick cooking spray and dust lightly with flour.

Combine the oil and sugar and beat until thick. Add the eggs, one at a time, and beat until smooth. Add the flour, salt, and baking soda. Mix in the apples, pecans, and vanilla. Pour the batter into the prepared pan and spread evenly.

Bake the cake 1 hour, or until it tests done. This is a very dense cake. Make sure the center of the cake is fully baked before removing it from the oven. Let the cake cool before turning onto a plate. If you choose to decorate this cake, warm a can of prepared lemon or vanilla frosting in the microwave for 45 seconds. Stir the frosting and drizzle it over the cooled cake, then decorate with pecan halves.

# GERMAN CHOCOLATE CAKE

You'll find that coconut pecan frosting makes this cake irresistible.

**Serves 18**

Preheat the oven to 350°F. Butter three 8-inch cake pans and dust lightly with flour.

Melt the chocolate in the top of a double boiler over boiling water. Cool.

Cream the butter and sugar until light and fluffy. Add the egg yolks, one at a time, beating after each addition. Add the vanilla and melted chocolate. Mix well. In another bowl, mix together the flour, baking soda, and salt. Add the flour mixture to the butter mixture alternately with buttermilk and beat until smooth.

Fold in the beaten egg whites carefully until the mixture is blended. Pour the batter into the prepared cake pans and bake 30 to 40 minutes, or until the layers test done. Cool the layers and freeze 1 hour before frosting them with coconut pecan frosting.

## Ingredients

1 box (4 ounces) Baker's German sweet chocolate

½ cup boiling water

1 cup (2 sticks) butter

2 cups sugar

4 egg yolks

1 tablespoon vanilla

2½ cups sifted cake flour

1 teaspoon baking soda

Pinch of salt

1 cup buttermilk

4 egg whites, stiffly beaten

1 can coconut pecan frosting

# CREAM PUFFS

## Ingredients

³/₄ cup water

¹/₂ teaspoon salt

¹/₃ cup unsalted butter, cut
into small pieces

³/₄ cup plus 2 tablespoons
flour

5 eggs

*H*ow lovely it is to bite into a delicate cream puff filled with custard or whipped cream. They are simple to make and quite elegant. This recipe is almost foolproof.

**Makes 36 cream puffs**

Preheat the oven to 400°F. Spray a cookie sheet with nonstick cooking spray or cover it with parchment paper.

Combine water, salt, and butter in a large pan. Bring the mixture just to a boil. Add the flour to the butter mixture all at once and beat with a wooden spoon.

Remove mixture from heat; continue to beat until it forms a ball. Return to very low heat and continue stirring for about 1 minute, or until the dough dries out somewhat.

Remove from the heat. Beat in 4 eggs one at a time, using a wooden spoon. The batter will become shiny. Place a metal tip with a large round opening into the bottom of a pastry bag. Press the dough out onto a cookie sheet about an inch apart, or drop pastry by the tablespoonful onto the prepared cookie sheet.

Glaze the puffs before baking. Mix an egg with a pinch of salt added and carefully brush onto the tops of the puffs. Gently press down on each puff with the tines of a fork to make a crossover pattern.

Bake 20 to 25 minutes, until the puffs are rounded and golden. Remove the cookie sheet from the oven and make a small slit in the side of each puff to release the steam. Allow the puffs to cool completely.

When the puffs are cool, split them in half and fill them with whipped cream, ice cream, custard, or pudding.

## Hint

To make eclairs, use a pastry tube and create a log shape about 3 inches long onto the cookie sheet. Proceed with instructions for cream puffs.

# TRIFLE

## Ingredients

3 cups whipping cream

1/2 cup powdered sugar

1 pound cake, or 4 cups
   cake scraps

1/4 cup liqueur, such as rum
   or Grand Marnier

1/2 cup water

1 box (7 ounces) French
   vanilla instant pudding

1 cup raspberry jam

3 large bananas, sliced

1 pint fresh raspberries

3 fresh peaches, sliced

*T*rifle is simple to prepare, dazzling to serve, and a great way to dispose of leftover cake. This is the thing to do with cakes that flop—thanks Nan! Feel free to change the fruit and the layering. Make your own custard or use a packaged mix.

**Serves 18 to 24**

You will need a deep glass bowl, about 6 inches deep and 8 to 10 inches across. Whip the cream until frothy. Add the powdered sugar and beat until stiff. Refrigerate.

Slice the pound cake into slices about the size of ladyfingers. Mix the liqueur and water. Dip each slice carefully in the liqueur-water mixture. Cover the bottom of the bowl with some of the sliced pound cake.

Prepare the pudding according to package directions and spread a layer over the cake. Drizzle some raspberry jam over the cake. Spoon a layer of fruit over the cake and spread about 1 inch of whipped cream over the top of the fruit.

Continue making layers alternately of pound cake, pudding, jam, fruit, and whipped cream until you have filled the bowl.

Refrigerate the trifle until serving time. Spoon into long-stemmed glasses; garnish with any remaining fruit and whipped cream.

# PEANUT BRITTLE

*L*ots of people need something sweet and crunchy to eat when they are anxious. This is an easy snack to make on a warm, dry day. The big secrets are to be very fast when you are pouring the mixture into the pans and to spread the candy as thin as possible using a spatula.

**Makes about 2 pounds**

Lightly oil 2 cookie sheets and set aside.

In a heavy 3-quart saucepan, stir together the sugar, water, and corn syrup. Stir constantly over medium-high heat, until the mixture comes to a boil and reaches 232°F on a candy thermometer.

Stir in the peanuts. Continue boiling; stir frequently until the mixture reaches 300°F.

Remove from the heat and stir in the baking soda, butter, and vanilla. *Quickly* pour onto the prepared cookie sheets and spread it as thin as possible using a spatula. Allow the candy to cool completely before breaking it into pieces.

## Ingredients

1 cup sugar

1 1/2 cups water

1 cup corn syrup

3 cups raw peanuts

1 tablespoon baking soda

1/2 cup (1 stick) butter, softened

1 tablespoon vanilla extract

# OH! NUTS!

## Ingredients

1 pound pecans,
   almonds, walnuts, or
   hazelnuts
2 egg whites
1 cup sugar
Pinch of salt
1 teaspoon cinnamon,
   optional
½ cup (1 stick) butter,
   melted

*T*his recipe came to me thanks to my lifelong friend, Betty Lias. The result is very professional despite the fact that they are easy to make. These are just like those candied pecans that cost $20 a pound. You will astound yourself.

**Makes 1¼ pound**

Preheat the oven to 325°F. Spread the nuts on a cookie sheet and bake 10 minutes, or until toasted. Pour the nuts onto another cookie sheet covered with several layers of paper towels.

While the nuts are cooling, beat the egg whites until stiff and fold in the sugar, salt, and cinnamon. Melt the butter in a microwave and brush it evenly on a cookie sheet.

Mix the nuts into the egg mixture and stir until the nuts are completely coated. Pour the nuts onto the prepared cookie sheet and stir until nuts are coated with the butter. Separate the nuts as much as possible.

Place the cookie sheet into the oven and bake 30 minutes, stirring every 10 minutes and separating the nuts. Make sure the nuts are completely covered with butter.

When the nuts are done, they will look dark and crunchy. Pour them onto the cookie sheet covered with paper towels to absorb any excess butter. When the nuts are completely cool, store them in an airtight container. These will keep for a long time. Put them in a fancy tin and they make a fabulous gift.

*For gingered meringue nuts:* Add 1 teaspoon of ginger in place of the cinnamon.

*For hot and spicy nuts:* Reduce the sugar to 1/2 cup and add 1/2 teaspoon chili powder, 1/2 teaspoon cayenne, 1 teaspoon garlic powder, a pinch of salt, 1 tablespoon soy sauce, and 1 tablespoon Worcestershire sauce. If you want these tongue-burning hot, increase the cayenne.

# SWEET AND SPICY NUTS

## Ingredients

2 cups nuts (pecans,
   walnuts, or hazelnuts)
1 egg white
1/2 cup sugar
1 teaspoon cinnamon
1 teaspoon vanilla or other
   flavoring

Another recipe thanks to Betty Lias. This time the butter is eliminated. The result is a nut with a thinner crust than the recipe for Oh! Nuts! but equally delicious. For an additional taste treat, add a teaspoon of orange flavoring.

**Makes 2 pounds**

Preheat the oven to 325°F. Spread the nuts on a cookie sheet and toast them for 10 minutes or until they are golden brown. Remove them from the oven and pour them onto a cookie sheet that is covered with several layers of paper towels. Lower the oven temperature to 300°F.

Beat the egg white until stiff and add the sugar, cinnamon, and flavoring. Stir the nuts into the meringue until they are well coated and spread them on a buttered cookie sheet, separating them as much as possible.

Bake for 40 minutes, turning the nuts every ten minutes and separating them as much as possible. Remove the nuts from the oven when they appear to be crunchy, and cool on paper towels.

Store in a jar with a tight-fitting lid. Tie a ribbon around the neck of the jar and you have a lovely hostess gift.

# MOMMA RITA'S EASY FUDGE

This recipe is easy and quick and almost foolproof. It works best on a day that isn't humid, but if it doesn't set up, you'll have fabulous fudge sauce.

**Makes 2½ pounds**

Butter an 8-inch square pan. In a microwavable bowl that holds at least 12 cups, mix the evaporated milk and sugar together. Microwave for 3 minutes on high. Stir and microwave another 3 minutes on high, until mixture reaches a full boil. Stir again and microwave an additional 2 minutes on high, until sugar is well dissolved and the mixture is foamy.

Place butter, vanilla, nuts, and chocolate chips in a large bowl. Pour the boiling mixture over them, and stir until very well mixed. Pour into the prepared pan, let cool, and enjoy!

## Ingredients

1 can (5 ounces) evaporated milk

2¼ cups sugar

½ cup (1 stick) butter, at room temperature

1 tablespoon vanilla

1½ cups chopped nuts of your choice

2 cups (12 ounces) semi-sweet chocolate chips

1 cup (6 ounces) milk chocolate chips

# CHOCOLATE TRUFFLES

## Ingredients

8 ounces fine semisweet
    chocolate, broken into
    small pieces
1 cup whipping cream, at
    room temperature
Melted chocolate and
    sweetened cocoa for
    dipping

## Hint

You can also pour the
ganache into a baking pan,
chill it until firm, cut it into
squares, and dip it in
melted chocolate. Use a
fondue fork to lift the
squares out of the choco-
late. Drop onto wax paper
and dry.

*N*obody knows the truffles I've seen, but this is
an easy recipe. All you need is an adventurous
spirit and cold hands. If your hands are always
warm, pat your hands with a cloth soaked in ice
water.

This is also known as *ganache* and is sensational used as filling and frosting for a cake or
torte.

**Makes 16 (1-ounce) truffles**

Using a microwave or double boiler, melt the
chocolate and cream together and mix until they
are well combined. Pour the mixture into a small
bowl and chill several hours, or even several
days, covered.

Shape the ganache into small balls using a
scoop or a spoon. Handle as little as possible and
remember to keep those fingers cold.

Refrigerate until ready to dip the truffles in
melted chocolate or roll in sweetened cocoa. *Do
not refrigerate* the truffles after they have been
dipped in chocolate or they will get sticky or
have white streaks. Keep them in a cool place at
65° to 70°F. Or, they can be frozen and thawed.

# CHOCOLATE BARK

*M*aking chocolate bark provides almost instant gratification because it is fast and easy. This should be fun for kids to make.

**Makes 2 pounds**

Line a cookie sheet with aluminum foil. Melt the chocolate chips together in the top of a double boiler. Stir the chocolate until it is smooth. Cool for 10 minutes. Stir nuts and optional white chocolate into the melted chocolate.

Add the raisins if desired and pour the mixture onto the prepared cookie sheet. Use a spatula to spread the chocolate to a thickness of about 1/4 inch.

Refrigerate 20 to 30 minutes until set and break into chunks.

*For white chocolate bark:* Replace the semisweet and milk chocolate with white chocolate; melt in the top of a double boiler over hot but not boiling water.

*For chocolate candy clusters:* Add mini marshmallows or peanut butter chips. Drop the mixture onto wax paper by the spoonful.

## Ingredients

6 ounces semisweet, milk chocolate, *or* white chocolate chips
6 ounces milk chocolate chips
1 tablespoon vegetable oil
1 cup chopped nuts
6 ounces white chocolate, optional
1/2 cup raisins, optional

## Hint

This is delicious if you substitute Rice Krispies or crisp Chinese noodles for the nuts.

# OVEN-BAKED CARAMEL CORN WITH NUTS

## Ingredients

5 quarts popped popcorn

2 cups salted peanuts, cashews, or pecans

1 cup (2 sticks) butter

2 cups firmly packed dark brown sugar

½ cup light corn syrup

*T*his is an exciting recipe because everyone loves caramel corn and you can make this in your oven—no more burned fingers using syrup. Break this up and it resembles the expensive snack you buy. Be sure to store it in an airtight container after it has cooled.

**Makes 5 quarts**

Preheat the oven to 250°F. Combine the popped corn and nuts in a large baking pan and place in the oven while the syrup is being made. Combine butter, brown sugar, and corn syrup in a heavy saucepan. A pinch of salt will accentuate the sweetness.

Cook and stir until the sugar dissolves. Bring mixture to a boil; cook until very thick and at the firm ball stage (a drop of syrup in a glass of water will form a firm ball), 260°F on a candy thermometer.

Remove the popcorn from the oven and pour the syrup over the corn and nuts. Mix well. Return the popcorn mixture to the oven and bake an additional 30 minutes. Stir every 10 minutes.

Remove from the oven and spread it on wax paper to cool, breaking it into small chunks. When completely cooled, store the caramel corn in an airtight container.

# CARAMEL PECAN TURTLES

*I*magine the delight of biting into caramel, chocolate, and pecans at the same time. These are the favorite comfort food of my grandsons Richard and Alexander.

**Makes 36 large or 60 small turtles**

Preheat the oven to 325°F. Spread the pecans on an ungreased cookie sheet and toast the nuts for 10 minutes. Remove the pan and cool the nuts completely.

In a heavy 2-quart saucepan, combine the sugars, salt, cream, and cream of tartar. Cook until the mixture reaches 238°F on a candy thermometer. Use a wet brush to wash down any sugar crystals that form on the side of the pan.

Remove pan from heat and allow the mixture to cool to 220°F. Add butter chunks and vanilla. Beat mixture until creamy and add pecans. Working quickly, drop the mixture by heaping tablespoonfuls onto the greased cookie sheets and allow to cool.

When the candies are hard, melt the semisweet chocolate and brush over the tops of the candies. Wrap the pieces in clear wrap and store in an airtight container.

## Ingredients

3 cups pecan halves

2 cups firmly packed light brown sugar

1 cup sugar

Pinch of salt

1 cup heavy cream

1/4 teaspoon cream of tartar

1/2 cup (1 stick) butter, cut into small bits

1 tablespoon vanilla

8 ounces semisweet chocolate

# EASY CARAMEL PECAN TURTLES

## Ingredients

1 pound pecans
1 pound caramels, unwrapped
8 ounces semisweet chocolate

**Makes about 2 dozen turtles**

Preheat the oven to 325°F. Spread 1 pound of pecans on an ungreased cookie sheet and toast the nuts for 10 minutes. Cool completely before using.

Place six pecans in a cluster, one for the head, one for the tail, and two each for the arms and legs of the turtle. Soften a caramel by kneading it with your fingers. Press a softened caramel onto the pecans. Brush the tops of the pieces with melted semisweet chocolate. Wrap the turtles individually in clear wrap, and store in an airtight container.

# FUDGE BALLS

Fudge balls were very popular at Chocoholics Bakery because we made them huge—about twice the size of a truffle and dipped them in milk chocolate. They are my granddaughter Ocea's all-time favorite candy.

**Makes 72 fudge balls**

## Ingredients

1 recipe Momma Rita's fudge (page 309)
2 cups (12 ounces) milk chocolate chips or artificially flavored chocolate coating
72 walnut halves

Prepare the fudge. After the fudge is cooled, cut it into squares and then work the fudge into a round ball.

Melt the milk chocolate chips in the top of the double boiler (not in a microwave). If using the artificial chocolate coating it can be melted in the microwave. Dip the individual fudge balls into the melted chocolate. Set them on wax paper to dry and decorate each fudge ball with a walnut half.

# MELT-IN-YOUR-MOUTH TOFFEE

## Ingredients

1 cup sugar

Pinch of salt

1/4 cup water

1/2 cup (1 stick) butter

1 cup chopped nuts of your choice

1 cup (6 ounces) chocolate chips

*T*his candy is not only crunchy and delicious but it actually melts in your mouth. Choose a dry, warm day to make this or it might be sticky.

**Makes 2 pounds**

Butter a cookie sheet. Using a heavy saucepan, combine the sugar, salt, water, and butter. Cook until the mixture reaches 270°F on a candy thermometer—the soft crack stage.

Stir in 1/2 cup of the nuts and pour immediately onto the prepared cookie sheet. Use a spatula to spread the candy out so that it is about 1/4 inch thick. Allow the candy to cool completely.

Melt the chocolate in the microwave for 2 minutes on high or until melted and spread it on top of the toffee. Sprinkle the remaining 1/2 cup nuts on top of the chocolate before the chocolate hardens. When the candy is completely cool, break it into pieces.

# ROCKY ROAD CANDY

*T*his candy is easy to make with your children or grandchildren. They will think you are a genius. I'm not sure whether we sold as much rocky road candy at the bakery as I ate, but here's the simple recipe. You can use a 1-pound candy bar or you can break up several small ones.

**Makes 2 pounds**

Milk chocolate is almost impossible to melt in a microwave, and it will burn. Use a double boiler and melt the chocolate over hot water.

Remove the chocolate from the heat and stir in the marshmallows and the nuts. Spread the mixture into a buttered 8-inch square glass baking dish or drop by the spoonful onto wax paper. Let the candy cool thoroughly before cutting into squares.

## Ingredients

1 pound milk chocolate

3 cups miniature marshmallows

1 cup chopped nuts of your choice

## Hint

You can use 3 cups of crisp Chinese noodles in place of the marshmallows and drop by the spoonful onto wax paper. Or, you can use crushed pretzels.

# BEVERAGES

Everyone has a drink that they consider part of their comfort food group. I've included lots of different beverages from hot cocoa to flavored coffees and, of course, time-honored mixed drinks that bring their own form of comfort.

Sip, guzzle, and slurp in good health.

# SPICED APPLE CIDER

*P*erfect to serve to yourself or a crowd on a chilly evening. This is a great hot drink for the holidays. If you serve this for an open house, your house will smell fantastic—especially if you bake cookies, too.

**Serves 18**

Combine all the ingredients except for the sugar in a large kettle and bring to a boil. Add the brown sugar and simmer for an additional 20 minutes.

Remove the cinnamon sticks, cloves, and all-spice and serve hot.

## Ingredients

3 quarts apple cider

10 cinnamon sticks

10 whole allspice

12 whole cloves

1 tablespoon ginger

3/4 cup firmly packed dark brown sugar

# OH! JULIUS!

## Ingredients

3 ounces frozen orange
   juice concentrate

$1/3$ cup milk

$1/2$ cup water

$1/4$ cup sugar

1 heaping tablespoon
   Carnation Instant
   Breakfast mix

4 ice cubes

*T*his is as close as possible to the drink you can buy at the mall. Vary the flavor by changing the fruit juice. We served lots of this drink at our dessert parlor. We called them smoothies and sometimes added ice cream and fresh fruit.

**Serves 2**

Use a blender to mix together all the ingredients. When the ice is completely crushed, serve this drink in tall frosted glasses.

# HOT CHOCOLATE MIX

*Ingredients*

3 cups powdered milk

¾ cup sugar

½ cup unsweetened cocoa

Pinch of salt

*H*ot chocolate is definitely comfort food. I prepared this for use at Chocoholics Dessert Parlor and eventually packaged and sold the mix for people to use at home. If you store this in a tightly sealed container, it will last indefinitely.

**Makes 4 cups of mix, enough for 16 (8-ounce) cups of hot chocolate**

Mix all the ingredients together. For each serving of hot chocolate, mix together 8 ounces of boiling water with ¼ cup of this mix. Top with whipped cream for a richer hot chocolate.

# MOCHA MIX

1 box (8-quart size) dry
    nonfat milk powder
2 cups sweetened cocoa
    powder
1 jar (6 ounces) nondairy
    creamer
1 jar (2 ounces) instant
    coffee crystals

## Hint

Eliminate the coffee
crystals to make hot chocolate mix.

*W*e sold lots of this drink at our dessert parlor.
It is easy to prepare in advance and requires only
the addition of boiling water.

**Makes 10 to 12 cups of hot mocha**

Combine all the ingredients and store in a
glass jar, tightly covered. Mix 3 heaping tablespoons (or to taste) of the mix into 1 cup hot
water and top with mini marshmallows.

# THICK CHOCOLATE MALT

## Ingredients

2 tablespoons chocolate
   syrup
1 tablespoon instant malted
   milk powder
1 pint ice cream, softened
Sweetened whipped cream
   for garnish

*I*f you eliminate the malted milk powder you will have a very rich milk shake. Is that a comforting idea?

**Serves 2**

Mix the chocolate syrup and the malted milk powder into the softened ice cream. Garnish with whipping cream.

# AQUA FRESCA (WATERMELON ICE)

## Ingredients

1 watermelon (4 pounds)
1 cup sugar, or to taste
1 quart shaved or finely
    chopped ice

## Hint

If you have simple syrup on hand (page 284), use 1 cup of simple syrup in place of the sugar. If the watermelon is very sweet, you may be able to eliminate the sugar.

*T*he first time I tasted this was in a little Mexican restaurant in San Francisco's garment district. It was served in a huge glass with crushed ice. There were even a few watermelon seeds but I was in total bliss. The restaurant is closed, but my memory of this drink goes on.

**Serves 8 to 12**

Remove the rind from the watermelon, cut into cubes, and remove the seeds. Use a blender to mix all the ingredients. Chill and serve.

# LEMONADE

What is more comforting than a glass of ice-cold lemonade on a hot day? If you roll the lemons on a hard surface before juicing them, you will get more juice. Freezing the juiced lemon for 30 minutes will make grating the rind easy.

**Makes 2½ quarts**

Boil the water and sugar until the sugar is completely dissolved. Cool the sugar syrup. Add the lemon juice and rind and stir well.

Pour into a large pitcher. Add the cold water and stir. Pour into large glasses filled with crushed ice and garnish with lemon slices and mint.

## Ingredients

1 cup water

1 cup sugar

1⅓ cups fresh lemon juice

Grated rind from 2 lemons

2 quarts ice-cold water

Lemon slices and mint for garnish

## Hint

Freeze some of the lemonade and when it is half frozen, mash it with a fork or blender and serve

# CHILDREN'S PUNCH

## Ingredients

2 cans (6 ounces each) frozen Hawaiian punch, defrosted

3 cups cold water

1 can (24 ounces) powdered lemonade mix

2 quarts chilled carbonated water

2 quarts chilled ginger ale

1 quart sherbet, any flavor

Kids love this drink, so make lots of it for a family reunion or a kids' birthday party.

**Serves 30**

Use a large punch bowl. Combine all the ingredients except for the sherbet and mix until well blended.

Cut the sherbet into chunks and add it to the punch. Serve immediately.

# EGGNOG

This is a Christmas holiday delight. Eliminate the booze or substitute flavorings and the kids will love it.

**Serves 25 to 30**

## Ingredients

12 eggs, separated
2½ cups sugar
4 cups bourbon
2 cups dark rum
4 cups milk
4 cups heavy cream, whipped
Grated nutmeg

Beat the egg yolks until thick and lemon colored. Add the sugar slowly. Add the bourbon, rum, and milk. Fold in the whipped cream. Whip the egg whites until stiff and fold them into the eggnog. Pour the mixture into a punch bowl. Sprinkle with grated nutmeg.

# GALLIANO

## Ingredients

2 cups distilled water

$1/2$ cup sugar

1 cup white corn syrup

$1 1/4$ cups grain alcohol
   (188 proof)

6 drops anise or licorice
   flavor

3 teaspoons vanilla

Several drops of yellow
   food coloring

*W*e used a great deal of liqueur at the bakery for baked goods as well as for flavoring whipped cream. These recipes were given to me by my loyal customers. Use these special liqueurs for your baking needs.

**Makes 1 quart**

Boil together the water, corn syrup, and sugar until the sugar is dissolved and well blended. Add the remaining ingredients and stir until well mixed. Pour into a jar with a tight fitting lid and store for at least a month before using.

# KAHLÚA

**Makes 8 cups**

Combine the water and the sugars and bring to a boil. Continue boiling this mixture until all the sugar is dissolved—about 5 minutes.

Remove the pot from the heat and cool for 15 minutes. Add the coffee, vodka, and vanilla.

Pour into a tightly capped jar and store for at least a month before using.

## Ingredients

2 cups distilled water

1½ cups firmly packed
   brown sugar

1 cup sugar

½ cup instant coffee

3 cups vodka

2 tablespoons vanilla

# CRÈME DE MENTHE

8 cups sugar

6 cups distilled water

1 pint grain alcohol,
    188 proof

1 ounce peppermint
    flavoring

6 drops of green food
    coloring

**Makes 8 cups**

Boil the sugar and water and simmer for 15 minutes. Cool the mixture and stir in the remaining ingredients.

Pour into a tightly sealed container and store the crème de menthe for at least a month before using.

# SANGRITA

If your idea of comfort food is liquid and alcoholic, this is deeply satisfying.

**Serves 8 to 10**

Mix all the ingredients together in a large pitcher. Pour the drink into ice filled glasses and decorate with lime slices.

## Ingredients

1 can (16 ounces) tomato juice

16 ounces orange juice

2 tablespoons fresh lime juice

4 ounces tequila

1 teaspoon Worcestershire sauce

Salt and pepper to taste

Tabasco sauce to taste

# SANGRÍA

## Ingredients

1 orange, sliced thin
1 lemon, sliced thin
¼ cup extra-fine sugar
½ gallon red Burgundy
½ cup orange-flavored
   liqueur
½ cup brandy
1 quart club soda

**S**erve this chilled in a pitcher for Sunday brunch and see how comfortable your guests will be.

**Serves 10 to 12**

Combine all the ingredients except for the club soda and let them blend together overnight.

Before serving, add crushed ice and the club soda. Stir well and serve.

# FROZEN DAIQUIRI

*T*his is so delicious and brings a great deal of comfort to even those who profess to dislike the taste of liquor.

**Serves 12 to 14**

Combine all the ingredients and freeze until almost frozen. Stir the mixture and spoon into cocktail glasses.

*Or* combine all the ingredients in a blender with crushed ice.

## Ingredients

1 can (6 ounces) frozen limeade

6 ounces water

18 ounces light rum

1 quart carbonated grapefruit soda

## Hint

If you use a blender or food processor, you can add a cup of any frozen fruit.

# HOT BUTTERED RUM

## Ingredients

1 cup (2 sticks) butter, at
    room temperature
1 pound dark brown sugar
$1/2$ teaspoon cinnamon
$1/2$ teaspoon nutmeg
$1/2$ teaspoon ground cloves
1 ounce dark rum per
    serving

*7he* flavor of butterscotch with a comfortable kick.

**Makes 2 cups rum mix, enough for 16 drinks**

Cream the butter and sugar together until well blended.

Add the seasonings and refrigerate. This will last a month in the refrigerator.

To serve, mix 1 tablespoon of batter with 6 ounces of boiling water and 1 ounce of dark rum.

# CHAMPAGNE PUNCH

This is a lovely way to serve champagne. As the frozen fruit mold melts, the flavor of the champagne is enriched. Consider making several small molds and floating them on the punch. Save this recipe for a wedding reception.

If you want to take the time to be artistic, freeze a small amount of the fruit mixture in the bottom of the mold. Place sliced fruit or flowers on the frozen portion and add a little liquid. When it is frozen, add the remaining fruit juices.

**Serves 40**

Place the bananas in a food processor or a blender, add a little pineapple juice, and purée.

Combine the sugar and water in a saucepan and heat until the sugar melts.

Add the fruit juice, lemon juice, pineapple juice, and banana purée and stir all the ingredients together.

Pour the mixture into a large ring mold and freeze.

When ready to serve the punch, unmold the fruit ring and place it in a punch bowl. Pour the champagne over it.

## Ingredients

4 ripe bananas

1 can (46 ounces) pineapple juice

3 cups sugar

6 cups water

2 cans (6 ounces each) frozen fruit juice concentrate, thawed

1 can (6 ounces) lemon juice concentrate, thawed

4 bottles (1 3/4 liters each) of champagne

## Hint

Use 4 quarts of ginger ale or lemon-lime soda to replace the champagne for a refreshing alcohol-free punch.

# MEXICAN COFFEE

## Ingredients

6 ounces brewed coffee
1 ounce Kahlúa
1 ounce light rum
1 teaspoon brown sugar
Whipped cream for garnish

*N*ew coffee shops open daily all over the country and the craze for flavored coffees is on. You can prepare the following recipes yourself at a fraction of the cost and enjoy them at home or take a carafe to the stadium with you. The directions are basically the same: Add the liqueurs and sugar to the coffee and decorate with whipped cream.

**Serves 1**

# GRASSHOPPER COFFEE

**Serves 1**

Add the liqueur and sugar to the coffee and stir. Add the ice cream and top with whipped cream if desired.

6 ounces brewed coffee

1 ounce crème de menthe

1 teaspoon brown sugar

1 scoop chocolate or vanilla
  ice cream

# IRISH CREAM

## Ingredients

1 can (14 ounces) sweet-
    ened condensed milk
1 pint heavy cream
3 eggs
3 tablespoons chocolate
    syrup
1 teaspoon coconut extract
1½ cups Irish whiskey

**S**erve this in coffee on St. Patrick's day.

**Makes 6 cups**

Use a blender and combine all the ingredients
except the whiskey. Add the whiskey and blend
again.

# INDEX